Back Bar Beer Figurines

George Baley

Schiffer Publishing Ltd
4880 Lower Valley Road, Atglen, PA 19310 USA

Dedication

This book is dedicated to Barb, Sassy, and Lucy, whose patience, support, and confidence made this adventure possible. Also, to my Mother, whose daily phones calls of encouragement made the project more bearable. And last, to all the good friends, living and deceased, who opened their homes, permitting this book to become a reality.

Library of Congress Control Number: 2001098924

Designed by "Sue"
Type set in Windsor BT/Korinna BT

ISBN: 0-7643-1526-9
Printed in China
1 2 3 4

Published by Schiffer Publishing Ltd.
4880 Lower Valley Road
Atglen, PA 19310
Phone: (610) 593-1777; Fax: (610) 593-2002
E-mail: Schifferbk@aol.com
Please visit our web site catalog at
www.schifferbooks.com
We are always looking for people to write books on new and related subjects. If you have an idea for a book, please contact us at the above address.

This book may be purchased from the publisher.
Include $3.95 for shipping.
Please try your bookstore first.
You may write for a free catalog.

In Europe, Schiffer books are distributed by
Bushwood Books
6 Marksbury Avenue
Kew Gardens
Surrey TW9 4JF England
Phone: 44 (0) 20 8392 8585
Fax: 44 (0) 20 8392 9876
E-mail: Bushwd@aol.com
Free postage in the UK. Europe: air mail at cost.

Contents

Preface

Back Bar Beer Figurines is a reference guide for collectors and dealers to identify, evaluate, and characterize what commonly are called back bar statues. It is directed toward figurines from more than 200 American breweries.

Acknowledgments

The compilation of a second generation book on the subject of back bar breweriana was a task that could not be completed without the participation of a large number of collectors and breweriana enthusiasts. The cooperation of those who permitted their collections to be photographed was critical to the completion of this project and is greatly appreciated.

A special thanks to Donna Baker, my editor, for her patience and guidance, and to Bruce Waters for all his photo tips. They helped make this a truly fun project.

Brian Anderson
Bob Arnold
John Beran
Paul Brady
Scott Bristol
Joe and Karen Carey
Bill Carlisle
Ed Cieslak
Chris and Paul Gust
Herb and Helen Haydock
John Paul Hudson
Norm Jay
Raynar Johnson
Bob and Rose Marie Junke
Bob Kates
Ron Kikta
Kent Knowles
Bill LaPenna
J.P. (Vic) Ligenza
Brian Noel
Carl Miller
Roger Owens
Keith Rosdahl
Don Roussin
John G. Schmidt
Rick Schmidt
Kent Speer
Charlie Staats
Gary Wick

Others:
Joseph Borowitz
Preston Bradshaw
Rod Everett
John Ferguson
Marv Gardner
Ken Hosteter
Bob Kay
Clinton Leonhardt
Don Schultz
Tom Snyder
John Williams

Introduction

To some collectors, back bar breweriana (BBB) is anything that goes behind the bar itself. That could include a myriad of items, including glasses, steins, coasters, foam scrapers, napkins, and a hundred more collectibles. For this presentation, the focus will be on domestic (United States) beer statues and small shelf signs whose depth exceeds approximately 3/4" and whose composition includes chalk, plastic, ceramic, metal, wood, latex, glass, and synthetic resins. Figural foam scraper holders (FSH) are included throughout the book as well as a few "go-with" items in the last chapter. The items shown encompass a period of about the last hundred years or so.

It is important to note some of the collectibles not included in this book. The list includes chalk wall hangings, whiskey and wine statues, non-figural foam scraper holders, "stuffed" figurines or dolls, and large mechanical floor displays like those from Hamm's and Lone Star. Hundreds of these items were also photographed and will be reserved for a future volume.

This volume is divided into eight chapters with the following format: Chapter One provides a brief historical perspective regarding point-of-purchase (POP) advertising. It also provides information on estimating the age of items, pricing, and grading. Chapter Two looks at the statue manufacturers and their manufacturing processes, along with a brief treatment on repairs and hints on detecting reproductions and fakes. Chapter Three, "The Main Event," contains the majority of the statues pictured and represents a wide array of types and styles. Interspersed among these statues are beer trays depicting the same theme used with some of the figurines. A kind of "go-with," they are a fun way to spruce up a collection of figurines. Chapters Four through Seven present selected topics, including Shelf Talkers and Misers, back bar scenes, hands holding containers, and barrels—the latter usually as banks. Chapter Eight briefly presents a few "go-with" items often collected by statue aficionados.

A unique number, followed by the brand name, brewery name, height in inches, material(s) of construction, and the vintage when used as point-of-purchase (POP) advertising, identifies each item pictured. Additional comments in the captions indicate rarity, clarifying information (e.g. lighted, special features about the pictured item, etc.), and lastly, a price range based on the characteristics discussed in the section on pricing. In addition, reference numbers are grouped in the index to identify the brewery.

Breweries sometimes employed identical statue styles, changing only the signs affixed to the item. This was especially true for many of the Blatz and Pabst statues where variations exist in wording, yet the basic item is the same. Also, some statues came in lighted and non-lighted versions based on state laws, marketing, or cost considerations. When multiple statues are known, and differ only by wording or lighted vs. non-lighted, the caption will indicate this by using the same reference number followed by a letter or letters. For example, the Hamm's bear 184 was issued as a packaged unit containing five different signs. This permitted bars to change the look of the item for different occasions. Rather than picture the same bear five times, the alternate signage versions are indicated by 184a, 184b, etc., along with the wording on the other signs.

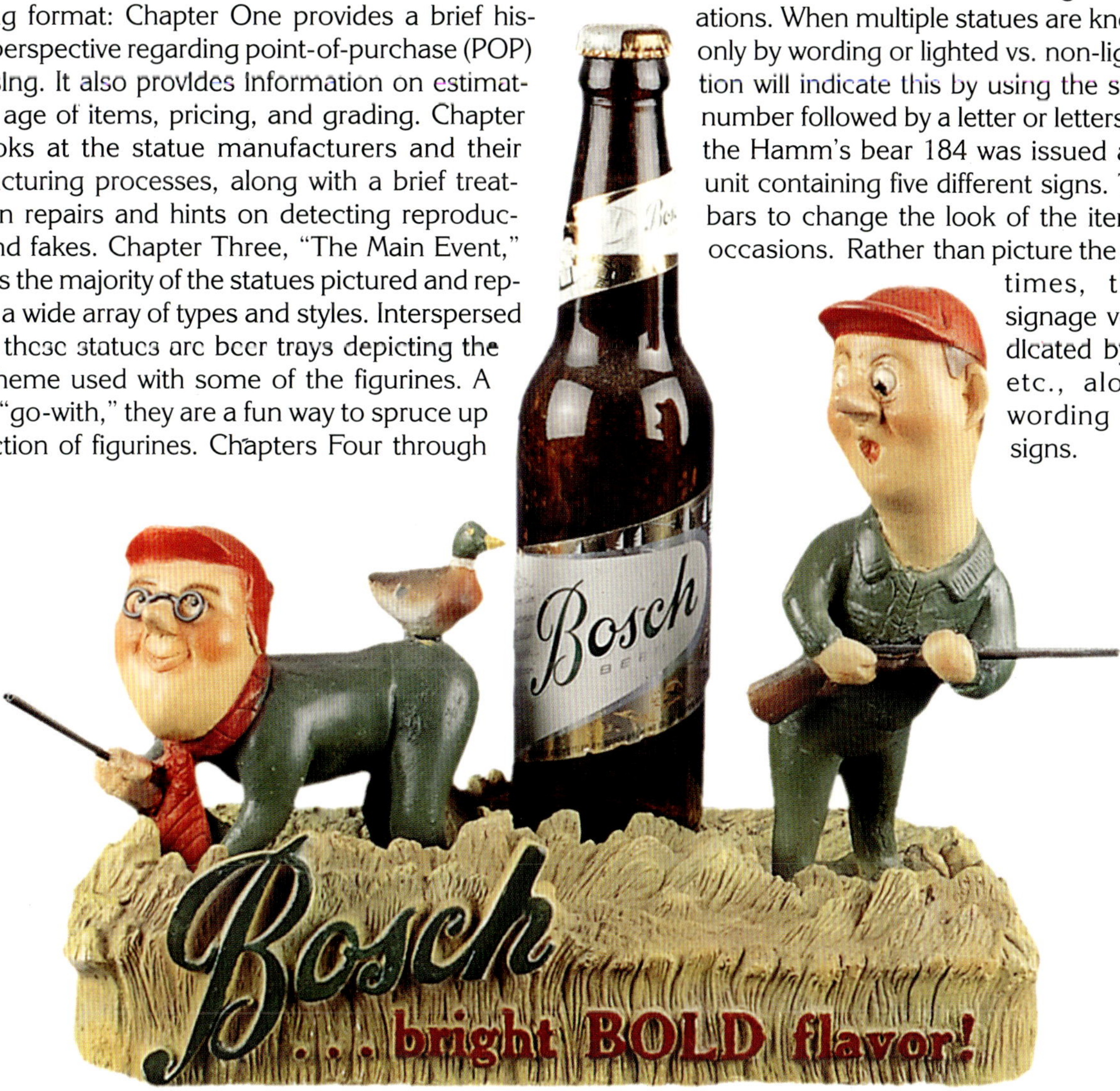

Chapter One: Point-Of-Purchase Displays

History

The first beer advertising dates back to the time of the ancient pyramids when beer was originally brewed. An Egyptian living alongside the Nile probably placed a sign in front of his pyramid and thus was born the first tavern! Subsequent to that time, numerous other forms of advertising were developed in an attempt to entice customers to imbibe in a glass of fermented hops.

Signs were the most common method of luring clients. The English pub, with its traditional hanging sign depicting the house brand of beer, continues in Great Britain to this day. A 1950s version of the old pub sign is this rare sign that hung in the tasting room of the Gettelman Brewery in Milwaukee, Wisconsin. It portrays a king-like person enjoying a glass of brew. Figurines were used as point-of-purchase (POP) displays for many non-beer related products during the nineteenth century; one only has to think of the cigar store Indian as an example from the past. As noted, the theme of this book will be on United States back bar breweriana, commonly referred to as "statues," and assorted smaller shelf signs called shelf talkers or shelf misers.

Figure 1. $1000 Sign from Gettelman.

BBB items were usually provided at no cost to bars and liquor stores that carried the brand advertised. Positioned in plain view of the customer and designed to entice purchase of the target product, they were special selling aids for beer salesmen, competing for shelf space behind the bar. What could be more appealing to a thirsty patron than viewing a handsome statue of one's favorite brew in the form of a chalk figurine as he or she sat at a bar, on a warm afternoon, after work?

The heyday for statues covered the period from post Prohibition years to the mid 1960s. This corresponds to a period in which beer consumption increased and brewery consolidation also accelerated. Regional brand loyalty was on the wane, as large national breweries like Anheuser-Busch, Coors, and Miller took a more aggressive position in gaining market share.

The Point-Of-Purchase Advertising Institute (POPAI), a Washington, DC based trade group, has created specific names to describe advertising displays. These include titles like Pole Topper, Dangler, Dump-Bin, Pre-Pack, Riser Card, Shelf Talkers, Shelf Misers, Dissolve, and Wobbler. In addition to the traditional statue, two popular types of back bar beer collectibles are the Shelf Talkers and Shelf Misers, which will be portrayed in Chapter Four. Shelf Talkers are small pieces characterized by many of the items from the Kolograph Company and are usually made of chalk. They were intended to fit on a back bar shelf and take up a minimum of space. Slightly larger, Shelf Misers take up more room than Talkers, but less than larger displays.

Boston Light Ale, an example of a Shelf Talker.

Wooden Shoe, an example of a Shelf Miser.

Estimating the Age

Collectors often ask, "What was the first true beer statue?" The answer depends on how collectors choose to define a statue. Many brands used figurals as brewery displays that were not provided to bars and taverns. These figurals often were made of brass, concrete, or granite and stood ten feet tall or more. The pot metal Schlitz (373) was likely a brewery figure and is identified with a copyright date of 1893. Another possible candidate is a metal figural clock of a St. Bernard (199) from The Highland Brewing Company of Springfield, Massachusetts, which dates from 1894 to 1899. The rare chalk/latex Carson Bock (80) from Carson City, Nevada appears to be from the early 1900s. The chalk Bull Frog (67) from United Breweries dates from 1898 to 1917 and comes closest to what is traditionally thought of as a beer statue.

With the earliest out of the way, let us consider techniques that may be helpful in dating this breweriana. Many of the popular brewery themes were employed for a number of years, making exact dating difficult. The best sources of information are actual brochures from statue makers like Plasto and W.J. Smith that depict the item in question. Portions of a full color brochure from Plasto are shown in Figure 2; this brochure dates from the 1940s and describes a wide variety of beer and non-beer figurines. Additionally, since some statues are identified with the name of the statue manufacture, checking old city phone books could prove helpful. *Life* or *Look* magazines highlighted new advertising campaigns. And, as shown in Figure 3, trade journals like *Spot Magazine* included an actual picture of the promotion for a new Blatz (30) baseball player statue. Matchbooks and coasters may offer clues to the date, especially if the name and address of the bar was included, as this information may be checked in phone books. Occasionally, a previous owner of the item may have written a date on the back or bottom to commemorate its receipt.

Figure 2. Plasto sales brochure.

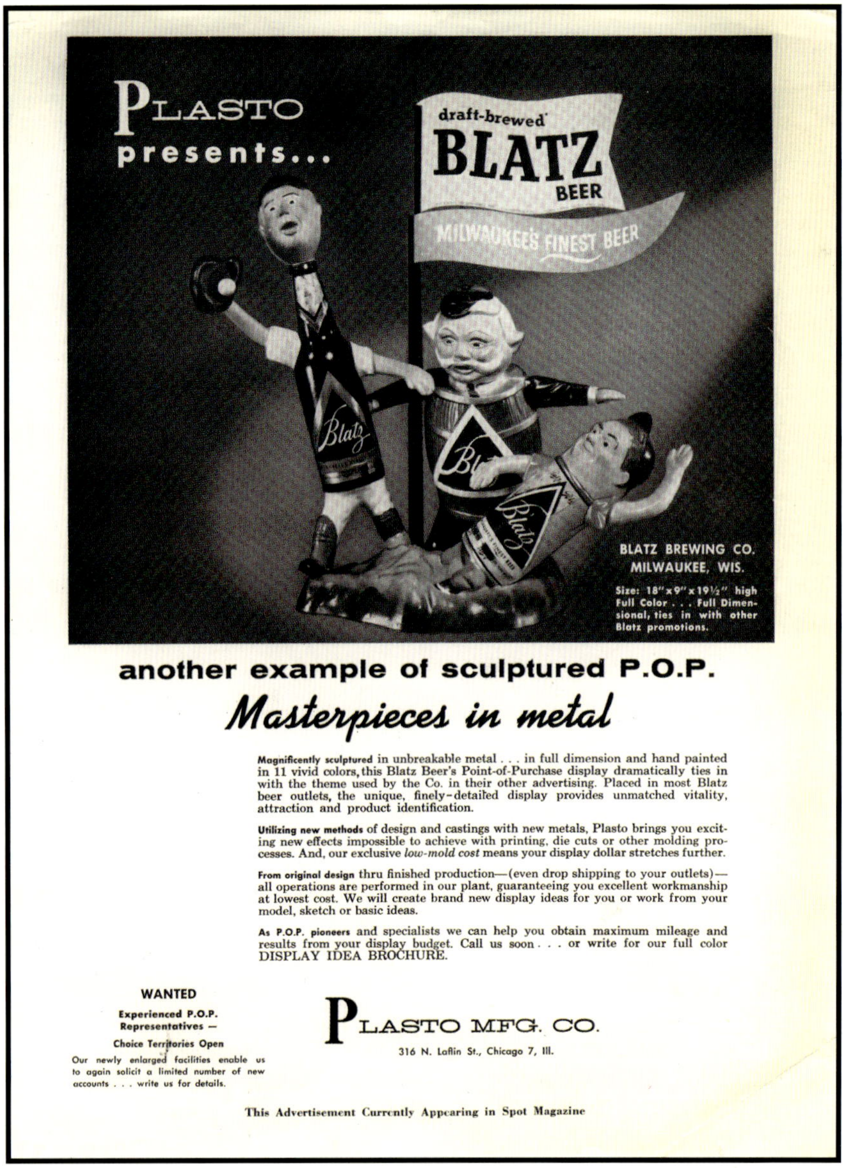

Figure 3. Plasto promo for Blatz statue.

Some breweriana includes a copyright date debossed or printed along with the brewery name and address. In many instances, the copyright date on the item is *not* the date it was manufactured since these dates are often found on items produced for many years. For example, the Utica Club bartender (417) has a reference to 1906 on the back, yet this is actually a 1940s foam scraper holder. Amazingly, sellers on Ebay of the Rolling Rock horse (357-359) statues claim their age to be the 1940s, when in reality these common statues were made in the 1960s. And lastly, the synthetic Leinenkugel hand (567) is often referenced on Ebay as being from the 1940s, when it actually was made in the late 1980s. Buyers beware!

Beer can or other breweriana related books are valuable dating resources by allowing comparison of a beer can or bottle label with the item in question. The collector should be aware that the can or bottle that is sold with the purchase of a statue might not be the correct one in use when the statue was manufactured. This is almost always the case when purchasing figurals that display a bottle or can. Thus, looking carefully at the print graphics, letter shape, size, or other symbols/logos on the statue itself may afford more meaningful clues than the beer bottle or can that is currently with the statue. During the 1950s, many beers that originally were spelled with an apostrophe "s" dropped the "s" from the spelling. Also, if the bottle or can contained the letters IRTP (Internal Revenue Tax Paid), it was made before 1950 when this legal requirement was discontinued. Verification of dates then becomes a challenge, much like participating in a good mystery game.

The Beer Can Collector's Bible, by Jack Martells, circa 1976, is the only beer can guidebook that provided dates for all U.S. cans described. In addition, brewery names and locations were included for both U.S. and foreign cans. Unfortunately, some of the dates are inaccurate, but it at least provides a target from which to start.

The New WHO'S WHO in Brew, prepared by John Vetter, circa 2000, is the most complete compilation of brands used between the end of Prohibition, April 1933, and about 1990. This reference is especially valuable when searching for brands produced between 1933 and 1970. The book summarizes by brand the type of beer, brewery, location, years produced, and the American Brewery code for more than 5000 brand names. To search a brewery location or dates of production, one needs to know only the label brand name.

American Breweries II, by Dale P. Van Wiersen, circa 1995, summarizes breweries in America by the brewery name and location. It does not provide a listing of brand names, but does an excellent job of summarizing virtually every brewery that existed in America by city and state and the dates of production.

Other quality reference books may be found in the bibliography section at the back of this book. This is by no means a complete listing of all books on the subject, but should serve as a good starting point for future work.

The four major breweriana collector groups in the U.S. publish periodic journals that contain many articles on various aspects of the hobby. The National Association of Breweriana Advertising (NABA) is focused primarily on non-beer can related collecting of both pre-prohibition and post-prohibition collectibles. The Beer Can Collectors of America (BCCA) primarily focuses on beer cans; although, in the past ten years a more general interest in breweriana collecting has developed. The American Breweriana Association (ABA) is heavily focused on newer collectibles, with an emphasis on collector mugs and mirrors. Each of these three associations has local chapters in various parts of the country. The Eastern Coast Breweriana Association (ECBA), as its name implies, tends towards east coast breweriana and more closely resembles the NABA in collector interests. Contact information for these groups may be found at the end of this book in Appendix A.

Pricing Statues

What determines the true value or worth of an item? Value is often measured by the old phrase, "beauty is in the eye of the beholder." At one time, I thought there were four characteristics in determining value: age, rarity, design, and condition. Now, after more than thirty years in the hobby, I have added a fifth: the online computer auction!

Unfortunately, over the past five years or so, with the advent of online computer auctions like Ebay the intrinsic worth of items (not just statues) has entered a new and undefined world. Twenty years ago, the thought of a statue being worth more than a hundred or so dollars was bizarre. Today, it is not uncommon for rare items to sell for upwards of $2000 or more! Perhaps one can accept the higher end, rare statues selling for extreme prices, but it is unnerving when low end, common statues are purported to be "rare" and demand excessive opening bids from unknowing or *unscrupulous* sellers.

That noted, let us look further at the first four characteristics in more detail.

Age is of importance since many collectors choose to focus only on statues of a particular vintage or brewery, e.g., the 1940s or 1950s. Thus, they concentrate their collecting on a more limited population that may be more expensive to obtain. Being older does not, however, equate to being rarer.

Rarity is a difficult attribute to quantify, due to the lack of accurate records concerning production quantities of statues. For example, the Plasto Company produced more statues than any other company in history. Orders of several thousand or more pieces for the very common Johnny Pfeiffer (317) each month made these the most common of all statues ever made. They were small and relatively inexpensive to make, costing the brewery somewhere around $0.35-0.50 each. Today, their collectible value is $25. Three vintage and similar size statues from Sebewaing (389-391) would likely have had the same manufacturing cost range, yet are extremely rare due to their very limited production. More expensive statues in the 1940s might have cost the breweries up to $3-5 each!

Imagine running a small brewery in the 1940s or early 1950s and trying to compete with the mega breweries like Anheuser-Busch, Miller, Pabst, or Blatz for back bar or package goods store advertising space. Perhaps your beer was sold in a very limited region of the country and your budget could not support the preparation of even a hundred statues, as may have been the case with the Sebewaing statues 389-391.

Since the cost to make small quantities of statues was prohibitive, it is likely the most rare of statues were either prototype test runs, or were intended for limited distribution to special customers and brewery executives. In my earlier book, it was suggested that to be "rare," six or less must be known to exist. One caveat to the number six is that in putting this book together many very nice collections, owned by persons not associated with any of the major collecting clubs, were discovered. Thus, while more than six of each of the most rare statues may actually exist, this number remains a good point of reference.

Design, to a large degree, impacts rarity. Statue manufacturers like Plasto employed a staff of six or more sculptors to design their products. Often these high quality and detailed statues were fragile and could not withstand rough handling, especially when they were removed from the back bar setting after their useful lives. The Bosch trifecta (52-54) is rarely seen intact because of the many small, fragile components. Likewise, the Van Merritt windmill (419) with its moving parts is usually found with nicks and dings.

Condition, condition, condition *should* affect the value of a statue, as it does with most other collectibles. I say *should*, with tongue in cheek, based on prices being paid for statues on the Internet and through transactions at collector shows. Because of their relative age and the fragile nature of chalk statues, few pristine examples have withstood the test of time. The section on restoration and repairs addresses the issue of how repairs affect the value of a statue. In the past twenty or so years, a number of "finds" of mint statues have occurred. Included in this group are the Gluek's (156), Kamm's (564), and Sterling girl (399). In time, more finds will undoubtedly be made.

Grading

Breweriana is normally graded by a system similar to that used for beer cans and defines a range from 1 to 5. At the end of each caption is a price range for the item pictured. This represents an expected range of value depending on different areas of the country and collector interest. The range shown would be for a statue in near perfect condition. Below is an interpretation of what percent of book a collector might apply to an item depending on its condition. For example, if an item is valued at a range of $100-150 and is estimated to be a Grade 3, the value range would be $60 to $120 depending on regional and collector interest.

Grade 1: (100% +) Pristine condition, free from chips, cracks, fading, or missing parts.

Grade 2: (80-100%) Very minor scratches, no chips, cracks, or missing parts.

Grade 3: (60-80%) Minor chips, no cracks, fading, or missing parts. Professionally repaired statues are classified as Grade 3.

Grade 4: (40-60%) Minor chips or cracks, slight fading, restorable missing parts. Non-professionally repaired/repainted statues are generally classified as Grade 4.

Grade 5: (0-40%) Large chips, cracks, and fading, restorable missing parts. Reserved for statues in extremely poor condition. Best used as a placeholder until a better example can be secured.

Chapter Two: The Manufacturers and More

In Chapter One, the first statue made was presented as uncertain based on a lack of documented history. Appendix B lists most of the known statue makers and, if known, the city where they were located. A large number of companies made and continue to make Shelf Misers.

The three premier companies making statues through the years were: the Plasto Manufacturing Company of Chicago, Illinois and W.J. Smith of Louisville, Kentucky for traditional statues and Kolograph of Los Angeles, California for Shelf Talkers. All are long gone, but the legacy they left requires special recognition.

Plasto, W.J. Smith, and Kolograph

Plasto Manufacturing

Plasto was started in Chicago in January 1944 by Joseph Borowitz in a 20' x 80' space on North Wells Street. Within months business was booming, so they moved to a 9000 sq. ft. factory on North Clyborn Avenue and increased their staff from two to fifty-five employees. By June of 1946 they again moved, this time into their final site, a six story 60,000 sq. ft. building on North Laflin (see Figure 4). Sales had grown from $30,000 in 1944 to over $300,000 in 1946. The high water mark for Plasto came in the 1960s when six full time sculptors and more than three hundred employees occupied the Laflin address. Both the second and third buildings still stand, although they now serve other tenants. Plasto made significant numbers of the Pfeiffer's, Bosch, Falstaff, Goebel, Old Reading, Drewrys, and Frankenmuth statues. Ironically, Joe Borowitz grew up in Louisville and was familiar with the local pottery tradition, yet never worked there for any of those companies, including the local W.J. Smith Company. Plasto was sold in 1984 to a conglomerate and moved to Kansas City where it filed for bankruptcy a few years later.

W.J. Smith Company

W.J. Smith was based in Louisville, Kentucky from the late 1930s to the 1960s. Their proximity to the large pottery trade in Louisville explains the natural involvement with statue making. W.J. Smith made most, if not all, the hands, wagon-like stand-ups (Griesedieck), Oertel's and WV snowmen, Altes, and many of the Falstaff statues under the title Plastica Displays.

Kolograph

Kolograph, based in Los Angeles, concentrated on Shelf Talkers and never made the traditional style or size statues. Dozens of Kolograph Talkers were made for a wide variety of non-beer products.

Figure 4. Plasto factory scene.

The Manufacturing Process

A statue manufacturer usually provided sample drawings of designs for consideration to the brewery. Once selected, a master prototype figure was prepared in clay by the statue company' s staff sculptors. Upon approval by the brewery, the clay version was used to fabricate a trial mold. In the early days of statue making, gelatin or "glue" molds were the common media used. Unfortunately, they limited the number of castings possible and tended to become malformed and unstable, especially in warm weather.

Nonetheless, a few plaster samples were cast, painted, and provided to the brewery prior to final approval of the production run. Samples of these brand-specific prototypes are rare and are represented by a few examples shown in Chapter Three, including the Miller girl (240), Patrick Henry (311), and Ortliebs (298). These nameless samples provided a level of secrecy to what was, at the time, a highly competitive field. Other nameless prototypes, like the rare generic hand (552) shown in Chapter Six, were presented to any brewery wishing to purchase a hand-type statue.

Once a sample was approved by the brewery, the manufacturer geared up for actual production. As mentioned, the early glue molds were made from gelatin and were limited in their ability to meet high production quantity needs. Because the drying action of plaster-of-paris is an exothermic reaction and generates heat, the glue molds required dipping in cold water between each casting to keep them cool.

In 1946, the Plasto Company, under the leadership of Joseph Borowitz, developed the first non-gelatin mold using a new material from the B.F. Goodrich Rubber Company called Korogel. A promotional ad for Plasto is shown in Figure 5. Unlike glue molds, this material was easier to use and lasted longer, which permitted more units to be manufactured per day. Korogel's rubber-like molds expanded the horizon of statue making at a time when this form of POP advertising was increasing in popularity.

Historically, plaster-of-paris was the common medium for statue making. Then in 1946, a material called Palestic was created in the Plasto labs to provide more durable figures that were less susceptible to breakage. Palestic was a combination of plaster-of-paris and bonding agents, plus added particles of fiberglass. The material was so much in demand that Plasto formed The Palestic Corporation and continued providing high quality material to many of the other statue companies for years.

To create the statues, the Palestic was combined with water and urea formaldehyde, mixed, and poured into the mold cavities. Figure 6 shows some interesting pictures of Plasto factory scenes. The casting was removed from the mold after about four hours. Next, workers scraped excess material from the seams and transferred the statues to the drying rooms. After drying, the figurines were moved to the finishing department for painting by hand or airbrush. Prior to the availability of infrared (IR) dryers, statues needed forty-eight hours to dry. With the advent of IR dryers, only six hours were required, thus permitting a statue to be completed in only twenty-four hours.

Figure 5. Plasto display brochure.

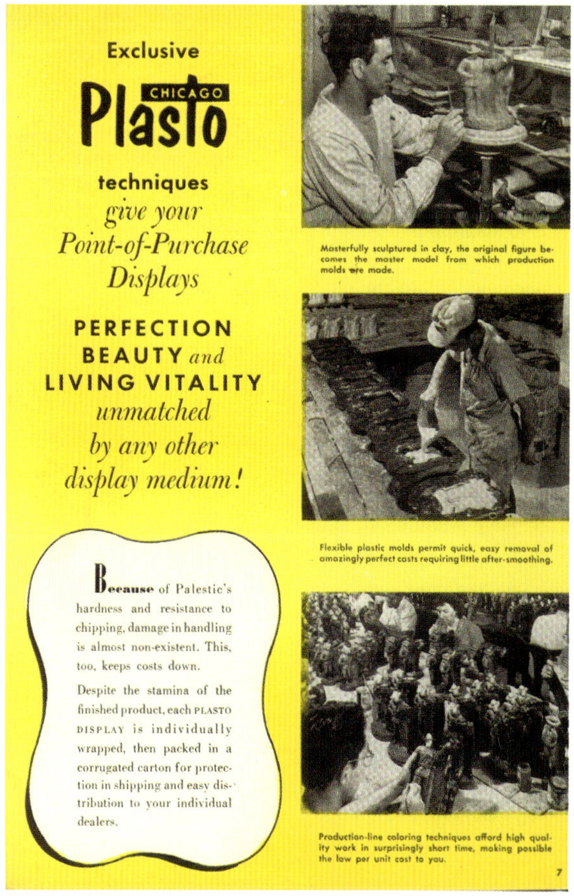

Figure 6. Plasto's production facility.

Shelf signs and flat style statues required a simple one-piece mold into which the casting material was poured. A rare, wax-like master of a Stoney's piece is shown in Figure 7. The master was used to prepare multiple mold cavities for casting production quantities. Shelf signs from Kolograph were cast in these simple molds, but required some machining to incorporate the characteristic sharp edges for which they are noted.

Figure 7. Stoney's master mold.

Three-dimensional statues, like the Falstaff (125) or West Virginia (426), required a two-piece mold to permit space between legs or arms. With today's injection molding technology, manufacture of plastic statues would be a simple task compared to the laborious nature of plaster castings in the old days.

Falstaff, Falstaff Brewing Co., 16.5" chalk, ca. 1954. $100-150. An example of a three-dimensional statue requiring a two-piece mold.

Because the molds were brand specific, manufacturers discarded them once the production requirements were met. With the exception of the pair of molds found to make the Oertels man (264) and hands discussed later in this chapter under reproductions, original molds are extremely rare today.

Other Materials of Construction

BBB has been manufactured employing a wide variety of materials, with plaster-of-paris being the most common. Hence, many collectors, when describing what they collect, use the nickname "chalks."

Metal

The first metal castings are represented by two Schlitz examples (372 and 373) and date to the turn of the last century. In the 1960s, the Plasto Company introduced a series of pot metal statues for Pabst and its newly acquired Blatz brewery. The Plasto Pabst and Blatz castings were fabricated by an outside mill, then shipped to Plasto for painting and final assembly. Because of their durable nature, most pot metal examples have held up well over the years, except for minor paint wear and scratching. Few of the pot metal examples are in great demand by collectors, other than those specializing in the specific brands represented. An exception is the desirable Blatz baseball players (30) coveted by sports collectors. Other breweries using metal were Piels (330), Valley Forge (418), Krueger (609), Schmidt's (379), and Sterling (399).

Ceramic

A limited number of ceramic statues were introduced, and were manufactured by companies who operated in the traditional chinaware/pottery arena. Examples include a series of Bull Dog (64-66), Burgermeister (71), Hamm's (various), My (619), and Old German (274). Undoubtedly, these were expensive to manufacture versus the relatively simpler chalk pieces. Many ceramics were made by McCoy and are often displayed in collector reference books for that manufacturer.

Latex/Rubber

A variety of latex or rubber-like statues have made their appearance over the years. Most likely easier to fabricate and less expensive than chalk, the rubber type statues never gained wide acceptance as POP displays in the brewery industry. Examples include Boston Ale (55), Buckeye (58), and Burger (68). While having the appearance of chalk, these statues were lighter in weight and did not afford the same degree of sturdiness, even though they better withstood breakage and chipping. Because of their rubber-like composition, heat became a serious problem with this type of statue and most examples found today show various degrees of deformity.

Plastic

As noted in the movie *The Graduate*, plastics were purported to be the wave of the future. In the POP arena, only a limited number of breweries accepted this form of material for their statues.

Polymer/Resin

An extremely hard, resin-like material was employed in the manufacture of the Bartender Joe, Lucky Guy, and Set 'em Up miniature bottle figures. It is interesting to speculate why this form of casting never received wider application. Perhaps cost was a factor?

Styrofoam

Styrofoam as a medium was employed for the Burgers (69 and 70), Falstaff (134a), Horlacher (204), Rainier (341), Schmidt's (385), and several others. The resulting product was even lighter in weight than the latex/rubber version, but was considerably less expensive to produce.

Wood

Wood never gained a popular place as a BBB medium with the exception of several shelf signs (501, 502, 508). The woodiest of the wood statues is the Heileman (197), a unique wood carved knight holding a stein of beer.

Glass

Glass as a medium was of limited application, probably due to cost, fragility, and a general lack of pizzazz. Examples include the Oertels (265) and Old Shay (290).

Cleaning and Repairs

The physical appearance and condition of a statue depends on the handling and storage conditions it has experienced during its lifetime. Since most are more than fifty years of age, it is remarkable to find very many in pristine condition.

The first treatment should be a gentle cleaning. Figurines, which spent their lives in smoky bars, are often found coated with an oily brown smoke residue. A dilute solution of liquid dish soap (similar to Lux), if applied with a dampened soft cloth or soft brush, will remove a significant amount of dust and grime. Avoid excessive use of water when cleaning chalk statues, since moisture can accelerate their decomposition. Gentle cleaning with rubbing alcohol (after testing for paint stability) may help remove stubborn smoke stains.

Cracks may be filled and missing parts fabricated with "Bondo," a fiberglass-like material.

If minor retouching is necessary, use of marking pens by "Sharpie" works especially well for black areas. Most colors require some experimentation to properly match the needed intensity. Generally, water based paints are more forgiving and permit rework, versus the more permanent solvent-based paints used for model airplanes. When the piece has been touched up, a final clear protective satin or semi-gloss spray finish offers a more durable surface and replaces the original sheen associated with statues.

Reproductions and Fakes

Fortunately, unlike some other areas of breweriana collecting, statues have been largely ignored as a target of reproductions. To date, reproductions from Oertel's are known to exist and are limited to the Oertel's man (264) often called "Howdy Doody" and an Oertel's hand. The authentic Oertel's hand (571) held a stubby bottle. The mold, however, was modified to permit it to hold a Crowntainer and is shown as statue 661.

The Oertel's right hand holding a 12-ounce bottle was authentic although a reproduction of 573 is being produced. The black Oertel's hand (660) is not authentic and is a painted version of the reproduction. The ashtray (662) never existed and is a fake fabricated from the base of the Oertel's man statue (264). These fakes continue to be made and sold in the Louisville area!

Both reproductions and fakes have the potential to become a serious problem. To the unsuspecting collector, unscrupulous persons may demand or suggest great value for statues that never were produced as breweriana. Oertel's reproductions can easily be detected by scratching the soft bottom with a coin or fingernail. The finish on the reproductions is dull and lifeless, unlike the crisp, shiny appearance of an authentic statue. In my first book, the Pitt's Ale (665) was at the time believed to be authentic and was erroneously placed in a prominent position on the back cover. This was later deemed to be a fake, a repainted non-beer generic statue of a decorative non-advertising nature. A more thorough search of the literature showed there never was a Pitt's brand beer! Other fakes and major repaints or mispaints continue to show up on Ebay over the past few years. Again, buyers beware!

New Collectibles

The proliferation of "new collectibles", during the past ten years, has resulted in a dramatic number of items being issued every month. Similar to the flourish of collectible beer cans and mugs in the 1970s, two clubs touting Budweiser and Hamm's are enmeshed in the proliferation of knick-knack type statues. I debated whether or not to include these new collectibles in this volume and after consultation with a number of senior collectors elected only to mention them. Thus, we will have to wait a bit longer to document the Budweiser frogs and numerous variety of Hamm's bear figurines—or leave them to another less discerning book.

Chapter Three: The Main Event

Many breweries developed themes consistent with the overall marketing strategy for the brand. Often themes were developed that continued to be used for years and became synonymous with the brand name. Concepts like the Hamm's bear, Drewry's Mounties, Sterling's bell girl, Fehr's bear, Rolling Rock's horse, Piel's Bert and Harry, the Johnnie Pfeiffer's soldier, Old Reading's Gus, Miller' s girl, Hanley's bulldog, Heidelberg's prince, Goebel's Bruster the rooster, the Schmidt's bartender, and on and on were carefully maintained in designing back bar pieces and other advertising.

Not every brewery took the time to develop a unique look to their advertising. The large number of generic hands and back bar scenes was promoted by statue manufacturers as a way to get a brewery's message out with the least amount of investment. This chapter features a wide variety of themes that, unlike the hands and barrels, are not easily grouped. The next few pictures illustrate some of the look-a-likes that were promoted by POP manufacturing companies. Different breweries that had no formal connection with each other employed similar statues.

Look-a-likes, as noted by the Crystal Rock-Gold Bond pair in Figure 8, are highly desirable chalk statues. The P.O.C.-Regal pair in Figure 9 are purported to have been issued at the time of the Republican and Democratic Conventions, a fact likely supported by the elephant and donkey that are mascots of the two parties. The Holihan's-Neuweiler pair in Figure 10 depicts the bartender pointing up the virtues of the named brand. As you flip through the following pages, see what other look-a-likes or near copycats you can some up with.

Figure 8. Crystal Rock-Gold Bond look-a-likes.

Figure 10. Holihan's-Neuweiler look-a-likes.

Figure 9. Regal-P.O.C look-a-likes.

1. A-1, Arizona Brewing Company, 11" chalk clock, ca. 1953. $750-1000.

4. Acme, Acme Breweries, 7" chalk, ca. 1940. $150-225.
4a. Acme, Acme Breweries, 6.75" molded latex, ca. 1940. $150-225. Not shown.

Right:
2. AB, Potosi Brewing Co., 12.5" chalk, ca. 1933-37. Rare. $500-750.

Below:
3. Acme, Acme Breweries, 7" chalk, ca. 1940. Reproduction are reportedly being made. $100-150 for authentic version, $10-15 for reproduction.

5. Acme, Acme Breweries, 13" chalk, ca. 1940. $250-375.

6. Alpine, Fox Deluxe Brewing Co., 11" chalk, ca. 1947. $150-225.

9. Alt Heidelberg, Columbia Breweries, 9" chalk, ca. 1950. $150-225.

10. Alt Heidelberg, Columbia Breweries, 9" chalk, ca. 1950. $150-225.

7. Alpine, Fox Deluxe Brewing Co., 16" chalk, ca. 1947. Lighted version may not be authentic. $150-225.

11. Altes, Altes Brewing Co., 9.5" chalk, ca. 1953. $100-150.

8. Alt Heidelberg, Columbia Breweries, 9" chalk, ca. 1946. $150-225.

12. Altes, Altes Brewing Co., 11" chalk, ca. 1953. $100-150.

13. Altes, Altes Brewing Co., 11" chalk, ca. 1953. Rare. $150-225.

14. Andeker, Pabst Brewing Co., 12" plastic, ca. 1965. $50-75.

15. Anheuser, Anheuser-Busch Inc., 12" plastic, ca. 1990s. $25-40.

16. Anteek, Charters Valley Brewery, 26" molded latex, ca. 1936-41. Rare. $1000+.

17. Apollo, American Brewing Co., 8.25" chalk, ca. 1933-43. $250-375.

Apollo tray.

20. Bankers, General Brewing Corp., 11" chalk, ca. 1948. $225-325.

18. Augustiner, August Wagner Breweries, 14" chalk, ca. 1935. Rare. $200-300.

19. Baltimore Brew, Baltimore Brewing Co., 17.5" metal, ca. 1933-36. Rare. $500-750.

21. Bankers, General Brewing Corp., 11" chalk, ca. 1948. $225-325.

22. Black Horse, Fred Koch Brewery, 8.5" plastic, ca. 1960. $10-20.
22a. Black Horse, Fred Koch Brewery, 8.5" plastic, ca. 1960. Black sign at bottom reads: "It's Totally Different." $10-20. Not shown.
22b. Black Horse, Fred Koch Brewery, 8.5" plastic, ca. 1960. White sign at bottom reads: "Thoroughbred of Ales." $10-20. Not shown.

23. Black Label, Carling Brewing Co., 15.5" chalk, ca 1968. $100-150.

24. Blatz, Blatz Brewing Co., 18.5" chalk, ca. 1936. $250-375.

25. Blatz, Blatz Brewing Co., 18.5" chalk, ca. 1937. $250-375.

26. Blatz, Blatz Brewing Co., 20" plastic, ca. 1984. $50-75.

28. Blatz, Blatz Brewing Co., 13.25" chalk, ca. 1965. $75-100.

29. Blatz, Blatz Brewing Co., 20" chalk/glass shade, ca. 1965. Rare lighted version. $150-225.

27. Blatz, Blatz Brewing Co. 13.25" chalk, ca. 1965. $75-100.

30. Blatz, Blatz Brewing Co., 16" metal, ca. 1965. $150-225.

31. Blatz, Blatz Brewing Co., 28" metal, ca. 1965. Original version used wood salt and pepper shakers. $225-325.

32. Blatz, Blatz Brewing Co., 17" plastic, ca. 1965. $75-100.
32a. Blatz, Blatz Brewing Co., 17" plastic, ca. 1965. This version has a lighted base. $85-125. Not shown.

33. Blatz, Blatz Brewing Co., 12" chalk, ca. 1960. Rare. $100-150.

Blatz tray.

34. Blatz, Blatz Brewing Co., 16" metal, ca. 1966. $75-100.

36. Blatz, Blatz Brewing Co., 11.5" plastic, ca. 1966. $35-50.

35. Blatz, Blatz Brewing Co., 18.5" metal, ca. 1968. $75-100.

37. Blatz, Blatz Brewing Co., 11.5" plastic/metal, ca. 1966. $35-50.

38. Blatz, Blatz Brewing Co., 11.5" plastic/metal, ca. 1966. Clock version. $50-75.

39. Blatz, Blatz Brewing Co., 10.5" metal, ca. 1966. $50-75.
39a. Blatz, Blatz Brewing Co., 10.5" metal, ca. 1966. Also came with clock. $60-90. Not shown.

40. Blatz, Blatz Brewing Co., 10.5" metal, ca. 1965. Clock version. $60-90.

41. Blatz, Blatz Brewing Co., 10.5" metal, ca. 1965. Clock version. $60-90.

42. Blatz, Blatz Brewing Co., 17" metal, ca. 1965. $75-100.

43. Blatz, Blatz Brewing Co., 17" metal, ca. 1965. Lighted version. $75-100.

44. Blatz, Blatz Brewing Co., 9" metal, ca. 1965. Clock version. $75-100.

47. Blatz, Blatz Brewing Co., 14" plastic/glass, ca. 1965. $25-40.

45. Blatz, Blatz Brewing Co., 9" metal, ca. 1965. Clock version. $35-50.

46. Blatz, Blatz Brewing Co., 14" plastic/metal, ca. 1965. $25-40.

48. Blatz, Blatz Brewing Co., 11" plastic/metal, ca. 1965. Sign lights and moves. Sign reads: "Now at Local Prices." $100-150.
48a. Blatz, Blatz Brewing Co., 11" plastic/metal, ca. 1965. Sign lights and moves. Also made with sign reading: "Milwaukee's Finest Beer." $100-150. Not shown.

49. Blatz, Blatz Brewing Co., 16" metal, ca. 1965. $35-50.
49a. Blatz, Blatz Brewing Co., 16" metal, ca. 1965. Also made with sign reading: "It's draft Brewed Blatz at Local Prices." $35-50. Not shown.

50. Blitz Weinhard, Blitz-Weinhard Co., 9" chalk, ca. 1951. $100-150.

51. Blitz Weinhard, Blitz-Weinhard Co., 9" chalk, ca. 1951. $125-175.

Blatz tray.

52. Bosch, Bosch Brewing Co., 10" chalk, ca. 1959. $750-1000.

53. Bosch, Bosch Brewing Co., 10" chalk, ca. 1959. $500-750.

54. Bosch, Bosch Brewing Co., 6.5" chalk, ca. 1959. $400-600.

55. Boston Light Ale, Boston Beer Co., 25" molded latex, ca. 1930s. Lighthouse has circulating beacon light. Rare. $500-750.

56. Breidt's, Peter Breidt Brewing Co., 17.5" metal, ca. 1934. Rare. $500-750.

57. Bruck's, Bruckmann Co., 11" ceramic, ca. 1937-49. Rare. $175-250.

58. Buckeye, Buckeye Brewing Co., 11.5" molded latex, ca. 1950. $60-90.

59. Bud Light, Anheuser-Busch Inc., 15" plastic, ca. 1987. Lights. $100-150.

60. Budweiser, Anheuser-Busch Inc., 15.5" plastic, ca. 2000. $125-175.

61. Budweiser, Anheuser-Busch Inc., 8" plastic, ca. 1970. $35-50.

Right:
62. Budweiser, Anheuser-Busch Inc., 6" metal, ca. 1990. $25-40.

63. Budweiser, Anheuser-Busch Inc., 21" plastic, ca. 1970. Distributor award in bronze. $100-150.
63a. Budweiser, Anheuser-Busch Inc., 21" plastic, ca. 1970. Distributor award in gold. $100-150. Not shown.
63b. Budweiser, Anheuser-Busch Inc., 21" plastic, ca. 1970. Distributor award in silver. $100-150. Not shown.

64. Bull Dog, Acme Breweries, 9" ceramic, ca. 1950s. $350-500.

65. Bull Dog, Acme Breweries, 9" ceramic, ca. 1950s. $350-500.

66. Bull Dog, Acme Breweries, 9" ceramic, ca. 1950s. $350-500.

Left:
67. Bull Frog, United Breweries, 24" chalk, ca. 1909. Rare. $750-1000.

68. Burger, Burger Brewing Co., 15" wood/latex, ca. 1952. $40-60.

69. Burger, Burger Brewing Co., 15" Styrofoam/latex, ca. 1959. $35-50.

70. Burger, Burger Brewing Co., 15" Styrofoam/latex, ca. 1963. $35-50.

73. Burgermeister, San Francisco Brewing Corp., 16" chalk, ca. 1953. $150-225.
73a. Burgermeister, San Francisco Brewing Corp., 16" chalk, ca. 1953. Similar to 73, but solid gold in color. $150-225. Not shown.

71. Burgermeister, Burgermeister Brewing Co., 8.5" ceramic, ca. 1971. $35-50.

72. Burgermeister, San Francisco Brewing Corp., 22.5" molded latex, ca. 1938. $175-250.

74. Burgermeister, San Francisco Brewing Corp., 16" chalk, ca. 1953. $150-225.

77. Busch, Anheuser-Busch Inc., 10.5" plastic/wood, ca. 1980. $25-40.

75. Burkhardt, Burkhardt Brewing Co., 7" chalk, ca. 1955. $125-175.

78. Canadian Ace, Canadian Ace Brewing Co., 10" chalk, ca. 1955. $150-225.

76. Busch, Anheuser-Busch Inc., 10" plastic, lights, ca. 1970. $25-40.

79. Canadian Ace, Canadian Ace Brewing Co., 8.5" chalk, ca. 1955. $250-375.

80. Carson Bock, Carson City Brewing Co., 20.5" molded latex/chalk, ca. 1915. Rare. $500-750.

Left:
81. Cavalier, Grace Bros. Brewing Co., 12" ceramic, ca. 1956-62. Rare. $250-375.

82. Chief Oshkosh, Oshkosh Brewing Co., 7" chalk, ca. 1950. $175-250.

Left:
83. Chief Oshkosh, Oshkosh Brewing Co., 11.5" chalk, ca. 1950. $225-325.

84. Cooper's, Cooper Brewing Co., 15" chalk, ca. 1946-48. No wording on side. $150-225.

85. Cooper's, Cooper Brewing Co., 15" chalk, ca 1946-48. Note wording: "Philadelphia, Pa" on side. $150-225.

86. Crystal Rock, Cleveland-Sandusky Brewing Corp., 13.5" chalk, ca. 1950. Rare. $500-750.

87. Delta, Delta Brewing Co., 8.5" molded latex, ca. 1933-39. Rare. $150-225.

88. Drewrys, Drewrys Ltd. USA, 25.5" chalk, ca. 1948. Rare. Probably from brewery boardroom. $1000+.

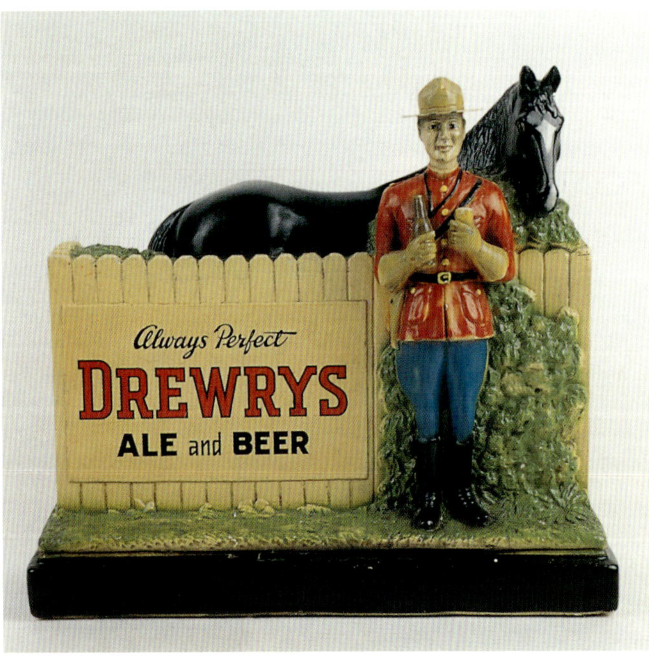

89. Drewrys, Drewrys Ltd. USA, 13" chalk, ca. 1950. Rare. $500-750.

90. Drewrys, Drewrys Ltd. USA, 15" chalk, ca. 1947. $225-325.

91. Drewrys, Drewrys Ltd. USA, 15" chalk, ca. 1947. $350-500.

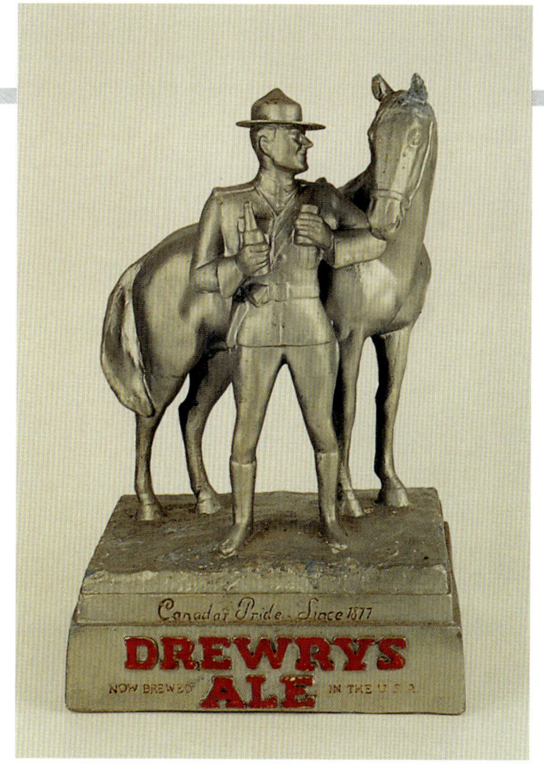

92. Drewrys, Drewrys Ltd. USA, 14" chalk, ca. 1953-58. Rare. $150-225.

94. Drewrys, Drewrys Ltd. USA, 27" chalk, ca. 1947. Lighted. Rare. $600-900.

93. Drewrys, Drewrys Ltd. USA, 16" chalk, ca. 1947. $500-750.

95. Drewrys, Drewrys Ltd. USA, 10.5" plastic, ca. 1950. Rare. $100-150.

98. Drewrys, Drewrys Ltd. USA, 7.25" chalk, ca. 1955. $25-40.

100. Drewrys, Drewrys Ltd. USA, 7.25" chalk, ca. 1955. $25-40.

96. Drewrys, Drewrys Ltd. USA, 11" chalk, ca. 1955. $50-75.

99. Drewrys, Drewrys Ltd. USA, 7.25" chalk, ca. 1955. $25-40.c

97. Drewrys, Drewrys Ltd. USA, 6.75" chalk, ca. 1955. $75-100.

101. Drewrys, Drewrys Ltd. USA, 7.25" chalk, ca. 1955. $25-40.

102. Drewrys, Drewrys Ltd. USA, 14.5" chalk, ca. 1955. Lighted. $100-150.

105. Drewrys, Drewrys Ltd. USA, 7" chalk ashtray, ca. 1947. Rare. $100-150.

106. DuBois, DuBois Brewing Co., 15.5" chalk, ca. 1960. $45-65.

103. Drewrys, Drewrys Ltd. USA, 11" plastic, with bottle, ca. 1957. $35-50.
104. Drewrys, Drewrys Ltd. USA, 11" plastic, with can, ca. 1957. $35-50.

107. DuBois, DuBois Brewing Co., 11" chalk, ca. 1945. $225-325.

110. Duquesne, Duquesne Brewing Co., 11" chalk, ca. 1956. $100-150.

108. DuBois, DuBois Brewing Co., 11" chalk, ca. 1945. $225-325.

Duquesne tray.

109. DuBois Budweiser, DuBois Brewing Co., 12.5" chalk, ca. 1960. $100-150.

111. Duquesne, Duquesne Brewing Co., 14.5" chalk, ca. 1956. $100-150.

112. Edelbrau, Edelbrau Brewery, 11.75" chalk, ca. 1960. $150-225.

Left:
113. Elfenbrau, C & J Michael, 20" chalk, ca. 1935. Rare. $750-1000.

114. Erin Brew, Standard Brewing Co., 4" chalk, ca. 1935. Rare. $150-225.

115. Erlanger, Otto Erlanger Brewing Co., 10" chalk, ca. 1945. $350-500.

116. Esslinger, Esslinger Inc., 19" chalk, ca. 1940. Rare. $750-1000.

117. Falls City, Falls City Brewing Co., 8.5" chalk, ca. 1953. $200-300.

118. Falls City, Falls City Brewing Co., 11" chalk, ca. 1953. $200-300.

Esslinger tray.

119. Falls City, Falls City Brewing Co., 8.5" chalk, ca. 1951. $175-250.

120. Falls City, Falls City Brewing Co., 11" chalk, ca. 1976. $150-225.

122. Falls City, Falls City Brewing Co., 10" plastic, ca. 1972. $25-40.

123. Falls City, Falls City Brewing Co., 9.5" metal, ca. 1950. $100-150.

121. Falls City, Falls City Brewing Co., 14" molded latex, ca. 1950. $75-100.

124. Falstaff, Falstaff Brewing Co., 11.8" chalk, ca. 1954. $75-100.

125. Falstaff, Falstaff Brewing Co., 16.5" chalk, ca. 1954. $100-150.

126. Falstaff, Falstaff Brewing Co., 21" chalk, ca. 1936. $350-500.

127. Falstaff, Falstaff Brewing Co., 21" chalk, ca. 1936. $350-500.

Falstaff tray.

128. Falstaff, Falstaff Brewing Co., 21" chalk, ca. 1936. $350-500.

130. Falstaff, Falstaff Brewing Co., 16.5" molded latex, ca. 1954. $50-75.

129. Falstaff, Falstaff Brewing Co., 16.75" chalk, ca. 1954. $150-225.

131. Falstaff, Falstaff Brewing Co., 8" molded latex, ca. 1948. $35-50.

132. Falstaff, Falstaff Brewing Co., 5" ceramic, ca. 1980. $35-50.

133. Falstaff, Falstaff Brewing Co., 8.5" chalk, ca. 1960. $25-40.

Left:
135. Falstaff, Falstaff Brewing Co., 10" plastic, ca. 1960. $50-75.

Right:
134. Falstaff, Falstaff Brewing Co., 8.5" chalk, ca. 1960. $25-40.
134a. Falstaff, Falstaff Brewing Co., 8.5" Styrofoam, ca. 1960. Also available in solid gold color. $25-40. Not shown.

136. Fehr's, Frank Fehr Brewing Co., 10.5" chalk, ca. 1953. $250-375.

Left:
137. Fehr's, Frank Fehr Brewing Co., 11" chalk, ca. 1954. $250-375.

138. Fehr's, Frank Fehr Brewing Co., 15.5" chalk, ca. 1953. $100-150.

141. Fox DeLuxe, Peter Fox Brewing Co., 16" chalk, ca. 1948. $350-500.

139. Fesenmeier, Fesenmeier Brewing Co., 8" chalk, ca. 1962. $75-100.

140. Fidelio, Fidelio Brewery, 9" chalk, ca. 1933-40. Rare. $250-375.

Fox DeLuxe tray.

142. Fox DeLuxe, Peter Fox Brewing Co., 11.5" chalk, ca. 1949. $400-600.

143. Fox Head 400, Fox Head Brewing Co., 9.75" chalk, ca. 1952. $75-100.

144. Frankenmuth, Frankenmuth Brewing Co., 8" composition, ca. 1950. $75-100.

145. Frankenmuth, Frankenmuth Brewing Co., 10" chalk, ca. 1951. $75-100.

Fox Head 400 tray.

146. Frankenmuth, Frankenmuth Brewing Co., 10" chalk, ca. 1951. $75-100.

149. Frankenmuth, Frankenmuth Brewing Co., 6" chalk, ca. 1946. $25-40.

150. Frankenmuth, Frankenmuth Brewing Co., 6" chalk, ca. 1946. $25-40.

147. Frankenmuth, Frankenmuth Brewing Co., 8" chalk, ca. 1948. Rare. $200-300.

148. Frankenmuth, Frankenmuth Brewing Co., 5.75" chalk, ca. 1946. $25-40.

151. Frankenmuth, Frankenmuth Brewing Co., 12.5" chalk, ca. 1962-65. $100-150.

152. Frankenmuth, Frankenmuth Brewing Co., 12.5" chalk, ca. 1962-65. $125-175.

153. Gettelman, A. Gettelman Brewing Co., 14.5" composition, ca. 1956. $75-100.

154. Gibbons, The Lion Inc., 8.5" chalk, ca. 1945. $150-225.

155. Gibbons, The Lion Inc., 11" chalk, ca. 1960. $225-325.

156. Gluek's, Gluek Brewing Co., 9.5" chalk, ca. 1959. $100-150.

157. Goebel, Goebel Brewing Co., 10.5" chalk, ca. 1955. $75-100.

158. Goebel, Goebel Brewing Co., 10.5" chalk, ca. 1955. $75-100.

159. Goebel, Goebel Brewing Co., 6" chalk, ca. 1955. $50-75.

160. Goebel, Goebel Brewing Co., 6" chalk, ca. 1955. Rare. $75-100.

161. Goebel, Goebel Brewing Co., 7" plastic, ca. 1960. $15-25.

162. Gold Bond, Cleveland-Sandusky Brewing Corp., 13.5" chalk, ca. 1940. Rare. $500-750.

163. Golden Glow, Golden West Brewing Corp., 12" chalk, ca. 1940. Rare. $1000+.

166. Griesedieck, Griesedieck Bros. Brewing Co., 10" chalk, ca. 1950. $125-175.

164. Grand Prize, Gulf Brewing Co., 10" chalk, ca. 1954. $250-375.

165. Grand Prize, Gulf Brewing Co., 10" plastic, ca. 1954. $50-75.

167. Gunther's, Gunther Brewing Co., 18.5" chalk, ca. 1938. Rare. $350-500.

168. Gunther's, Gunther Brewing Co., 12" molded latex, ca. 1957. $350-500.

171. Hals, Hals Brewing Co., 2.5" chalk, ca. 1952. $20-30/pair.

173. Hamm's, Theo Hamm's Brewing Co., 12" ceramic bank, ca. 1959. $150-225.

169. Hals, Hals Brewing Co., 2.5" chalk, ca. 1952. $20-30/pair.

172. Hamm's, Theo Hamm's Brewing Co., 12" ceramic bank, ca. 1959. The brown bear bank is rare. $250-375.

170. Hals, Hals Brewing Co., 2.5" chalk, ca. 1952. $20-30/pair.

174. Hamm's, Theo Hamm's Brewing Co., 12" ceramic bank, ca. 1959. $150-225.

175. Hamm's, Theo Hamm's Brewing Co., 11" ceramic decanter, ca. 1973. $25-40.

176. Hamm's, Theo Hamm's Brewing Co., 10.75" ceramic decanter, ca. 1973. $25-40.

178. Hamm's, Theo Hamm's Brewing Co., 6" ceramic, ca. 1970. $25-40.

Hamm's tray.

177. Hamm's, Theo Hamm's Brewing Co., 10.75" ceramic decanter, ca. 1973. $25-40.

179. Hamm's, Theo Hamm's Brewing Co., 19" ceramic lamp, ca. 1970. Rare. $125-175.

180. Hamm's, Theo Hamm's Brewing Co., 11" ceramic, ca. 1973. $30-45.

182. Hamm's, Theo Hamm's Brewing Co., 15.5" plastic calendar, ca. 1968. $75-100.

181. Hamm's, Theo Hamm's Brewing Co., 16.5" plastic, ca. 1970. $50-75.
181a. Hamm's, Theo Hamm's Brewing Co., 16.5" plastic, also with sign reading: "Bartender serving Hamm's," ca. 1970. $50-75. Not shown.

183. Hamm's, Theo Hamm's Brewing Co., 15.5" plastic, ca. 1968. $50-75.

184. Hamm's, Theo Hamm's Brewing Co., 20.5" Styrofoam, ca. 1970.This statue came packaged with a variety of sign choices in addition to the one shown. $40-60.
184a. Hamm's, Theo Hamm's Brewing Co., 20.5" Styrofoam, ca. 1970. Came with sign reading: "Hamm's ON TAP." $40-60. Not shown.
184b. Hamm's, Theo Hamm's Brewing Co., 20.5" Styrofoam, ca. 1970. Came with sign reading: "Hamm's AMERICA'S CLASSIC PREMIUM BEER." $40-60. Not shown.
184c. Hamm's, Theo Hamm's Brewing Co., 20.5" Styrofoam, ca. 1970. Came with sign reading: "Hamm's THE BEER REFRESHING." $40-60. Not shown.
184d. Hamm's, Theo Hamm's Brewing Co., 20.5" Styrofoam, ca. 1970. Came with sign reading: "SEASON'S BEST." $40-60. Not shown.

185. Hampden, Hampden Brewing Co., 15" chalk, ca. 1947. $100-150.

Hampden tray.

186. Hanley's, James Hanley Co., 9.5" chalk, ca. 1930s. $200-300.

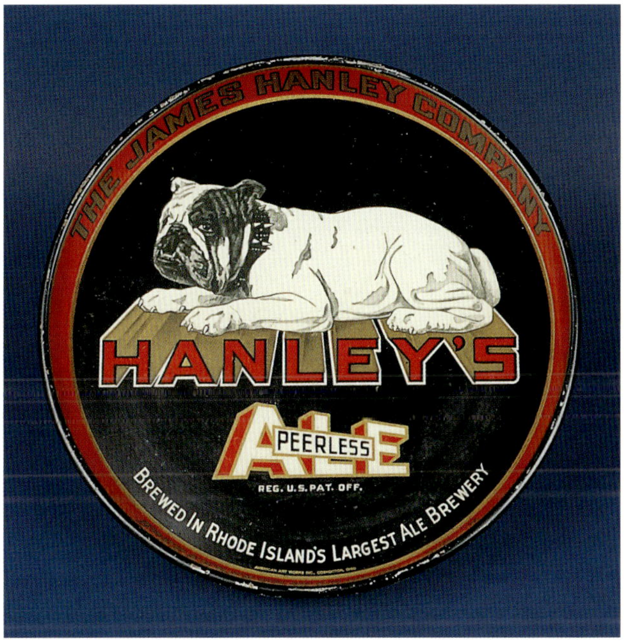

Hanley's Ale tray.

188. Hanley's, James Hanley Co., 9.5" cast iron, ca. 1930s. $275-400.

187. Hanley's, James Hanley Co., 9.5" chalk, ca. 1930s. $225-325.

189. Hanley's, James Hanley Co., 9.5" cast iron, ca. 1948. $275-400.

190. Hazelton, Pilsener Brewing Co., 12" latex, ca. 1938. Rare. $500-750.

191. Heidelberg, Heidelberg Brewing Co., 9" chalk, ca. 1952-58. $150-225.

192. Heidelberg, Heidelberg Brewing Co., 6" chalk, ca. 1952-58. $150-225.

193. Heidelberg, Heidelberg Brewing Co., 13.5" chalk, ca. 1948. $100-150.

195. Heidelberg, Heidelberg Brewing Co., 8.5" chalk, ca. 1955. $25-40.

196. Heidelberg, Heidelberg Brewing Co., 8.5" chalk, ca. 1955. $25-40.

197. Heileman's, G. Heileman Brewing Co., 19" wood, ca. 1940. $150-225.

194. Heidelberg, Heidelberg Brewing Co., 13.5" chalk, ca. 1948. $100-150.

198. Hensler, Joseph Hensler Brewing Co., 6" molded latex, ca. 1945. Rare. $500-750.

199. Highland, Highland Brewing Co., 15" metal clock display, ca. 1895. Rare. $500-750.

200. Hofbrau, Hofbrau Brewing Co., 11" chalk, ca. 1948. $200-300.

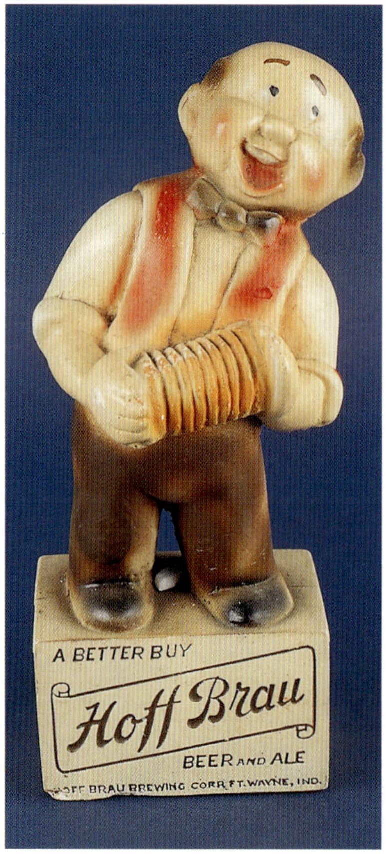

Left:
201. Hoff Brau. Berghoff Brewing Co., 10" chalk, ca. 1951-54. $100-150.

Below:
202. Hoff's, Johann, 24" chalk, ca. 1925. A rare example of a statue from a supplier of malt extract to the brewery industry. Rare. $300-450.

203. Holihan's, Diamond Spring Brewery, 12" plastic, ca. 1950. $100-150.

204. Horlacher, Horlacher Brewing Co., 10.5" Styrofoam, ca. 1960. Statue correctly displays a quart bottle. $225-325.

205. Hudepohl, Hudepohl Brewing Co., 9" chalk/plastic, ca. 1953. $225-325.

206. Hudepohl, Hudepohl Brewing Co., 9" chalk/plastic, ca. 1953. $350-500.

207. Hudepohl, Hudepohl Brewing Co., 12.5" chalk, ca. 1955. $250-375.

208. Hudepohl, Hudepohl Brewing Co., 16" chalk, ca. 1960. $60-90.
209. Hudepohl, Hudepohl Brewing Co., 16" chalk, ca. 1960. $60-90.

211. Hudepohl, Hudepohl Brewing Co., 12.5" chalk, ca. 1942-1944. A rare patriotic statue supporting the WW II efforts. $350-500.

210. Hudepohl, Hudepohl Brewing Co., 15" chalk, ca. 1965. $150-225.

212. Hyde Park, Hyde Park Breweries Assn., 14" chalk, ca. 1950. Rare. $250-375.

213. Imperial, Ajax Brewing Co., 15" chalk ca. 1939-41. Rare. $1000+.

214. Iroquois, Iroquois Beverage Co., 16" chalk, ca. 1960. "Iroquois Brewery" stamped in ink on bottom. $350-500.

Imperial tray.

Iroquois tray.

215. Iroquois, Iroquois Beverage Co., 6" hard rubber (far left), ca. 1945. $50-75.
216. Iroquois, Iroquois Beverage Co., 6" hard rubber (second from left), ca. 1945. $60-90.
217. Iroquois, Iroquois Beverage Co., 6" hard rubber (second from right), ca. 1945. $50-75.
218. Iroquois, Iroquois Beverage Co., 6" pot metal (far right), ca. 1945. $50-75.

219. Iroquois, Iroquois Beverage Co., 9" Styrofoam, ca. 1955. $125-175.

221. Jax, Jackson Brewing Co., 16.5" plastic, ca. 1958. Lights. $175-250.

220. Jax, Jackson Brewing Co., 9" molded latex, ca. 1946. Rare. $225-325.

222. King Kole, King Brewery, 6.5" chalk, ca. 1939-41. $300-450.

223. Koehler's, Erie Brewing Company, 7.5" chalk, ca. 1960. $150-225.

224. Kuebler, Kuebler Brewing Co., 10" chalk, ca. 1950. $500-750.

226. Lemp, Wm. J. Lemp Brewing Co., 20.5" chalk, ca. 1935/may be pre-pro. Rare. $1000+.

225. Leisy's, Leisy Brewing Co., 5" chalk, ca. 1945. Rare. $150-225.

227. Lion, Lion Brewery of New York City, 16" chalk, ca. 1933-41. $400-600.

228. Lion, Lion Brewery of New York City, 8.5" chalk, ca. 1940. $225-325.

231. Lite, Miller Brewing Co., 5" ceramic bank, ca. 1990. $35-50.
231a. Lite, Miller Brewing Co., 5" ceramic bank, ca. 1990. Same as 231, but nose and fins are white. $35-50. Not shown.

229. Lion, Lion Brewery of New York City, 8.5" chalk, ca. 1940. $225-325.

232. Lite Ice, Miller Brewing Co., 14" plastic, ca. 1998. $20-30.

230. Lion, Lion Brewery of New York City, 9" chalk, ca. 1950. $200-300.

233. Lone Star, Lone Star Brewing Co., 22" Styrofoam, ca. 1980. $50-75.

234. Lone Star, Lone Star Brewing Co., 12" chalk, ca. 1958. $75-100.

235. Lucky, General Brewing Corp., 11.5" chalk, ca. 1950. $175-250.

236. McSorley's, Liebmann Breweries, 9" latex, 1933-46, $200-300.

237. Michelob, Anheuser-Busch Inc., 24" plastic, ca. 1966. Lights. $100-150.

238. Michelob, Anheuser-Busch Inc., 24" plastic/wood, ca. 1966. Lights. $100-150.

239. Michelob, Anheuser-Busch Inc., 15" plastic, ca. 1966. Lights. $75-100.

240. Miller, Miller Brewing Co., 14.75" chalk, ca. 1950. Prototype for the Miller Girl statues. Note the unusual paint scheme. Rare. $150-225.

Miller tray.

241. Miller, Miller Brewing Co., 14.75" plastic (far left), ca. 1950. $60-90.
242. Miller, Miller Brewing Co., 14.75" chalk (second from left), ca. 1950. $100-150.
240. Miller, Miller Brewing Co., 14.75 chalk (center), ca. 1950. Prototype for the Miller Girl statues. Rare. $150-225.
243. Miller, Miller Brewing Co., 14.75" chalk (second from right), ca. 1950. $100-150.
244. Miller, Miller Brewing Co., 14.75" plastic (far right), ca. 1950. $60-90.

245. Miller, Miller Brewing Co., 6" plastic (far left), ca. 1950. $20-30.
246. Miller, Miller Brewing Co., 6" plastic (second from left), ca. 1950. $10-15.
247. Miller, Miller Brewing Co., 6" plastic (center), ca. 1950. $20-30.
248. Miller, Miller Brewing Co., 6" plastic (second from right), ca. 1950. $10-15.
249. Miller, Miller Brewing Co., 6" plastic (far right), ca. 1950. $20-30.
250. Miller, Miller Brewing Co., 6" brass, appears like 246/249, but is solid brass, ca. 1950. $30-45. Not shown.

251. Miller, Miller Brewing Co., 12" plastic, ca. 1950. $75-100.

252. Mug Ale, Burkhardt Brewing Co., 6.75" chalk, ca. 1940. $50-75.

253. Mustang, Pittsburgh Brewing Co., 10.5" plastic/wood, ca. 1970. $50-75.

Left:
254. Narragansett, Narragansett Brewing Co., 9.5" glass/latex, ca. 1960. $10-20.

Below:
255. National Bohemian, National Brewing Co., 6" chalk, ca. 1948. $250-375.

256. National Bohemian, National Brewing Co., 9.5" metal, ca. 1953. Driver's award for meritorious service. $125-175.

Right:
258. National Bohemian, National Brewing Co., 10" wood/latex, ca. 1950. $100-150.
258a. National Bohemian, National Brewing Co., 10" wood/latex, ca. 1950. Also available with a can. $100-150. Not shown.

259. National Bohemian, National Brewing Co., 8" plastic/ latex, ca. 1950. $100-150.
259a. National Bohemian, National Brewing Co., 8" plastic/ latex, ca. 1950. Also available with a bottle. $100-150. Not shown.

257. National Bohemian, National Brewing Co., 7" chalk, ca. 1950. $175-250.
257a. National Bohemian, National Brewing Co., 7" chalk, ca. 1950. Also available with a can. $175-250. Not shown.

Right:
260. Neuweiler, Louis F. Neuweiler's Sons, 12" plastic, ca. 1960. $100-150.

261. Oertels, Oertel Brewing Co., 14.25" chalk, ca. 1950. $225-325.

263. Oertels, Oertel Brewing Co., 13" chalk, ca. 1954. $225-325.

262. Oertels, Oertel Brewing Co., 14.75" chalk, ca. 1954. $150-225.

264. Oertels, Oertel Brewing Co., 16.25" chalk, ca. 1955. Statue pictured is authentic. However, this statue is being reproduced. Referred to as the "Howdy Doody" statue. $150-225 for authentic version; $50-75 for reproduction.

265. Oertels, Oertel Brewing Co., 9" glass, ca. 1954. $75-100.

267. Old Brew, Garden City Brewery, 12" chalk, ca. 1945. $500-750.

266. Old Appleton, Appleton Brewing Co., 12" chalk, ca. 1940-47. Rare. $225-325.

268. Old Crown, Centilivre Brewing Corp., 10" chalk, ca. 1946. Rare. $250-375.

269. Old Dutch, Krantz Brewing Corp., 12" chalk, ca. 1938. $1000+.

270. Old Dutch, Krantz Brewing Corp., 12" composition, ca. 1952. $100-150.

271. Old Dutch, Krantz Brewing Corp., 12" composition, ca. 1952. $125-175.

272. Old Export, Cumberland Brewing Co., 14" chalk, ca. 1960. $175-250.

273. Old Export, Cumberland Brewing Co., 13" chalk, ca. 1960. $225-325.

274. Old German, Queen City Brewing Co., 5.5" ceramic, ca. 1950. $100-150.

275. Old German, Queen City Brewing Co., 5" ceramic, ca. 1950. $175-250.

276. Old German, Queen City Brewing Co., 12" plastic, ca. 1965. $75-100.
276a. Old German, Queen City Brewing Co., 12" plastic, ca. 1965. Lighted version. $75-100. Not shown.

279. Old Imperial, Rahr Green Bay Brewing Co., 12" chalk, ca. 1940. $225-325.

280. Old Imperial, Rahr Green Bay Brewing Co., 12" chalk, ca. 1940. $225-325.

277. Old German, Queen City Brewing Co., 14" chalk, ca. 1952. $250-375.

278. Old German, Queen City Brewing Co., 12" chalk, ca. 1960. $100-150.
278a. Old German, Queen City Brewing Co., 13.5" Styrofoam, ca. 1960. $75-100.

281. Old Reading, Old Reading Brewery, 12" chalk, ca. 1957. $225-325.

283. Old Reading, Old Reading Brewery, 12.5" chalk, ca. 1957. $150-225.

282. Old Reading, Old Reading Brewery, 12" chalk, ca. 1957. $225-325.

284. Old Reading, Old Reading Brewery, 23.5" chalk, ca. 1957. Lighted version may not be authentic. $75-100.

Old Shay tray.

285. Old Reading, Old Reading Brewery, 12" chalk, ca. 1957. $125-175.

286. Old Shay, Fort Pitt Brewing Co., 11" chalk, ca. 1950. $100-150.

287. Old Shay, Fort Pitt Brewing Co., 11" chalk/latex, ca. 1950. $100-150.

288. Old Shay, Fort Pitt Brewing Co., 19" chalk/latex, ca. 1950. Lighted version may not be authentic. $75-100.

290. Old Shay, Fort Pitt Brewing Co., 9" glass, ca. 1948. $135-200.

289. Old Shay, Fort Pitt Brewing Co., 10.5" plastic/latex, ca. 1960. $75-100.

291. Old Style, G. Heilman Brewing Co., 24" latex, ca. 1930s. Rare. $1000+.

292. Old Tap, Enterprise Brewing Co., 9.5" chalk, ca. 1939. $275-400.

294. Old Timers, Cleveland-Sandusky Brewing Corp., 12" chalk, ca. 1955. $125-175.

Old Tap tray.

295. Old Timers, Cleveland-Sandusky Brewing Corp., 12" chalk, ca. 1955. $125-175.

293. Old Timer, West Bend Lithia Co., 6" chalk, ca. 1950. Rare. $225-325.

296. Old Timers, Cleveland-Sandusky Brewing Corp., 12" chalk, ca. 1955. $125-175.

298. Ortliebs, Henry F. Ortlieb Brewing Co., 16.5" chalk, ca. 1945. Rare prototype for Ortliebs statue #299. $150-225.

297. Olde Towne, Consumers Brewing Co., 9.25" chalk, ca. 1945. $200-300.

299. Ortliebs, Henry F. Ortlieb Brewing Co., 15.5" chalk, ca. 1945. $350-500.

300. P.O.C., Pilsener Brewing Co., 10.25" chalk, ca. 1952. Purported to be a political convention item. See Regal statue #352 for a look-a-like. $125-175.

302. Pabst, Pabst Brewing Co., 10" chalk pretzel holder, ca. 1955. $150-225.

303. Pabst, Pabst Brewing Co., 10.25" chalk, ca. 1937. Man holds a beer can. Rare. $1000+.
303a. Pabst, Pabst Brewing Co., 10.25" chalk, ca. 1937. Came in version of man holding a tray and bottle. Rare. $1000+. Not shown.

301. Pabst, Pabst Brewing Co., 14" chalk, ca. 1952. Model for this statue was purported to be Doris Day. $150-225.

304. Pabst, Pabst Brewing Co., 11" metal, ca. 1960. $100-150.
304a. Pabst, Pabst Brewing Co., 11" metal, ca. 1960. Also available with sign reading: "ON TAP." $100-150. Not shown.
304b. Pabst, Pabst Brewing Co., 11" metal, ca. 1960. Also available with sign reading: "ENJOY OLD TIME FLAVOR." $100-150. Not shown.

305. Pabst, Pabst Brewing Co., 13" metal, ca. 1950. Lighted. $125-175.
305a. Pabst, Pabst Brewing Co., 13" metal, ca. 1950. Lighted. Also available with sign reading: "ENJOY OLD TIME FLAVOR." $125-175. Not shown.

306. Pabst, Pabst Brewing Co., 14" metal, ca. 1960. Unusual version with only one mug on arm compared to 316. $75-100.
306a. Pabst, Pabst Brewing Co., 14" metal, ca. 1960. Unusual version with only one mug on arm compared to 316. Also available with sign reading: "ENJOY OLD TIME FLAVOR." $75-100. Not shown.

Pabst tray.

307. Pabst, Pabst Brewing Co., 14" metal, display includes the original ON TAP sign, ca. 1960. $85-120.

308. Pabst, Pabst Brewing Co., 11" metal, ca. 1960. $60-90.
308a. Pabst, Pabst Brewing Co., 11" metal, ca. 1960. Also came with a clock in place of the sign. $60-90. Not shown.

309. Pabst, Pabst Brewing Co., 11" metal/plastic, ca. 1965. $50-75.

310. Pabst, Pabst Brewing Co., 16" Styrofoam, ca. 1970. $30-45.

311. Patrick Henry, Fox Deluxe Brewing Co., 9.5" chalk, ca. 1952. Rare prototype for statues 312 and 313. $100-150.

Left:
312. Patrick Henry, Fox Deluxe Brewing Co., 10.75" chalk, ca. 1952. $600-900.

313. Patrick Henry, Fox Deluxe Brewing Co., 10.75" chalk, ca. 1952. $250-375.

314. Patrick Henry, Fox Deluxe Brewing Co., 13" Styrofoam, ca. 1952. Rare. $75-100.

Right:
315. Pearl, Pearl Brewing Co., 7.5" chalk, ca. 1940. Rare. $100-150.

316. Pete's Wicked Ale, Minnesota Brewing Co., 8" plastic nodder, ca, 1990s. $20-30.

317. Pfeiffer's, Pfeiffer Brewing Co., 7.25" chalk, ca. 1952. $25-40.

318. Pfeiffer's, Pfeiffer Brewing Co., 7.25" chalk, ca. 1952. $25-40.

319. Pfeiffer's, Pfeiffer Brewing Co., 10.75" chalk, ca. 1952. $80-120.

321. Pfeiffer's, Pfeiffer Brewing Co., 13.5" chalk, ca. 1952. $100-150.

320. Pfeiffer's, Pfeiffer Brewing Co., 10.75" chalk, ca. 1952. $50-75.

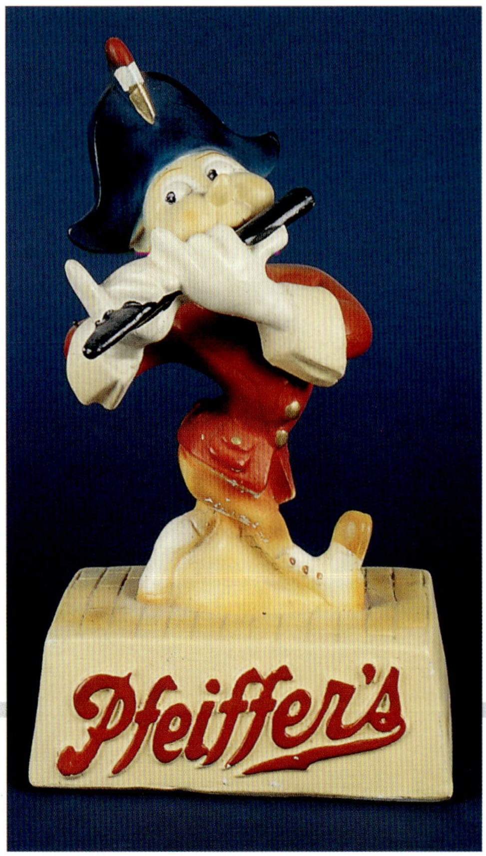

322. Pfeiffer's, Pfeiffer Brewing Co., 13" chalk, ca. 1952. Arms move. Rare. $150-225.

323. Pfeiffer's, Pfeiffer Brewing Co., 14.5" chalk, ca. 1952. $125-175.

325. Phoenix, Phoenix Brewing Co., 10" chalk, ca. 1946. $750-1000.

324. Pfeiffer's, Pfeiffer Brewing Co., 15" chalk, ca. 1952. $150-225.

326. Phoenix, Phoenix Brewing Co., 10" chalk, ca. 1946. This rare statue came from the President of Phoenix's office. Note color differences from 334. $800-1000.

327. Pickwick, Haffenreffer & Co., 14" molded latex, ca. 1959. $100-150.

328. Piels, Piels Bros., 10.5" chalk, ca. 1950. $125-175.

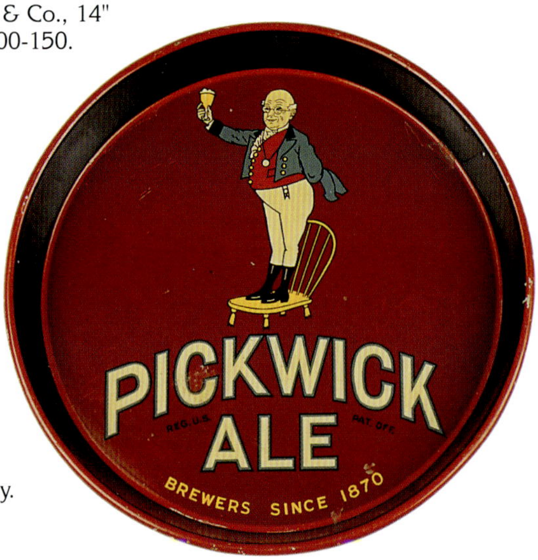

Pickwick Ale tray.

329. Piels, Piels Bros., 12" molded latex, ca. 1960. Bert & Harry were widely used on Piels advertising. $50-75.

329a. Piels, Piels Bros., 12"molded latex, ca. 1960. Also came with a stubby bottle. $50-75. Not shown.

Piels tray.

330. Piels, Piels Bros., 9.5" metal, ca. 1960. $100-150.

332. Piels, Piels Bros., 5" molded latex, ca. 1945. $35-50.

Piels tray.

333. Piels, Piels Bros., 4" molded latex, ca. 1944. $150-225.

331. Piels, Piels Bros., 8" metal, ca. 1960. $50-75.

334. Pilsener, Cream City Brewing Co., 10" chalk, ca. 1933-39. Rare. $250-375.

335. Pioneer, Pioneer Brewing Co., 11" chalk, 1933-44. Rare. $1000+.

Left:
336. Poth, Poth Brewing Co., 18" chalk, ca. 1936. Rare. $1000+.

337. Prior, Adam Scheidt Brewing Co., 6" plastic FSH, ca. 1945. $25-40.

338. Probst, Mound City Brewing Co., 24" ceramic, ca. 1946. Rare. $750-1000.

339. Rainier, Sicks Rainier Brewing Co., 16" chalk, ca. 1946. $250-375.

340. Rainier, Sicks Rainier Brewing Co., 16" composition, ca. 1956. $150-225.

341. Rainier, Sicks Rainier Brewing Co., 16" Styrofoam body/composite head, ca. 1956. $125-175.

Right:
342. Rainier, Sicks Rainier Brewing Co., 7.5" chalk, ca. 1955. $750-1000.

343. Rainier, Sicks Rainier Brewing Co., 15" chalk, ca. 1955. $150-225.

344. Rainier, Sicks Rainier Brewing Co., 8" chalk, ca. 1955. $150-225.

345. Rainier, Sicks Rainier Brewing Co., 13.5" chalk, ca. 1955, Rare. $250-325.

346. Rainier, Sicks Rainier Brewing Co., 10" ceramic, ca. 1995. $25-40.

347. Red Fox, Largay Brewing Co., 15" stone like material, ca. 1936. Rare. $1000+.

348. Red Top, Red Top Brewing Co., 14" latex/wood, ca. 1948. $225-325.

349. Red Top, Red Top Brewing Co., 13" latex/wood, ca. 1948. $225-325.

351. Red Top, Red Top Brewing Co., 13" chalk, ca. 1952. Rare. $500-750.

350. Red Top, Red Top Brewing Co., 13" chalk, ca. 1952. $350-500.

352. Regal, Drewrys Ltd. USA, 10" chalk, ca. 1952. Purported to be a political convention item. See P.O.C. statue #300 for a look-a-like. $150-225.

353. Renner, Renner Company, 7.5" chalk, ca. 1946. $150-225.

354. Renner, Renner Company, 12" molded latex, ca. 1948. Rare. $250-375.

355. Rheingold, Liebmann Breweries, 12" chalk, ca. 1946. Rare. $750-1250.

356. Rheingold, Liebmann Breweries, 11.5" Styrofoam, ca. 1970. $25-40.

357. Rolling Rock, Latrobe Brewing Co., 11" chalk (left), ca. 1970. $10-20.
358. Rolling Rock, Latrobe Brewing Co., 10.75" chalk (center), ca. 1970. $10-20.
359. Rolling Rock, Latrobe Brewing Co., 11" chalk (right), ca. 1970. $10-20.

360. Rolling Rock, Latrobe Brewing Co., 11" chalk, ca. 1970. Unusual in that horse has thinner legs than the common #359. $35-50.

Below:
361. Rolling Rock, Latrobe Brewing Co., 18" chalk, ca. 1960. $275-400.

362. Rolling Rock, Latrobe Brewing Co., 19" molded latex, ca. 1960. Rare. $275-400.

363. Rolling Rock, Latrobe Brewing Co., 9" plastic, ca. 1950. $225-325.

364. Rolling Rock, Latrobe Brewing Co., 14" chalk, ca. 1960. $200-300.

365. Rolling Rock, Latrobe Brewing Co., 14" chalk, ca. 1960. $200-300.

368. Ruppert, Jacob Ruppert, 10" chalk, ca. 1940. $150-225.

366. Ruppert, Jacob Ruppert, 9" chalk, ca. 1940. Rare. $150-225.

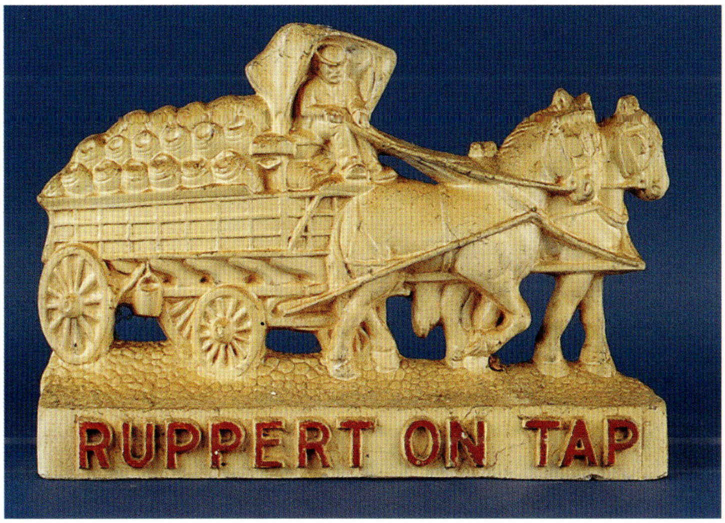

367. Ruppert, Jacob Ruppert, 10" chalk, ca. 1940. $150-225.

369. Schaefer's, F & M Schaefer Brewing Co., 14" plastic, ca. 1960. $25-40.

370. Schell's, August Schell Brewing Co., 8" chalk, ca. 1950. $150-225.

Below:
371. Schlitz, Jos. Schlitz Brewing Co., 32" chalk, ca 1930-40. Rare. $750-1000.

372. Schlitz, Jos. Schlitz Brewing Co., 25" metal, ca. 1930-40. Rare. $500-750.

373. Schlitz, Jos. Schlitz Brewing Co., 20" metal, ca. 1900s. $500-750.

374. Schlitz, Jos. Schlitz Brewing Co., 36" chalk, ca. Pre-pro. Rare. $750-1000.

375. Schlitz, Jos. Schlitz Brewing Co., 5" ceramic, 1974. $25-40.

376. Schlitz, Jos. Schlitz Brewing Co., 12.5" plastic/metal lamp, ca. 1960. $50-75.

Right:
377. Schlitz, Jos. Schlitz Brewing Co., 45" plastic, ca. 1960. Lights. $75-100.

378. Schmidt, Jacob Schmidt Brewing Co., 3.5" plastic, ca. 1960. $25-40.

380. Schmidt's, C. Schmidt & Sons, 8.25" metal FSH, ca. 1950. $20-30.

382. Schmidt's, C. Schmidt & Sons, 13" metal FSH, ca. 1950. $50-75.

379. Schmidt's, C. Schmidt & Sons, 8.25" metal FSH, ca. 1950. $10-20.

381. Schmidt's, C. Schmidt & Sons, 13" chalk FSH, ca. 1950. $50-75.

383. Schmidt's, C. Schmidt & Sons, 13" molded latex FSH, ca. 1950. $50-75.

384. Schmidt's, C. Schmidt & Sons, 8.5" chalk, ca. 1950. $100-150.

386. Schott, Schott Brewing Co., 11" chalk, ca. 1934-1935. Issued by brewery to thank President Roosevelt for ending Prohibition. Rare. $350-500.

385. Schmidt's, C. Schmidt & Sons, 15" Styrofoam, ca. 1968. $60-90.

387. Sebewaing, Sebewaing Brewing Co., 8" chalk, ca. 1946. $250-375.

388. Sebewaing, Sebewaing Brewing Co., 9.5" chalk, ca. 1947. $150-225

389. Sebewaing, Sebewaing Brewing Co., 4" chalk, ca. 1955. Rare. $100-150.

390. Sebewaing, Sebewaing Brewing Co., 4" chalk, ca. 1955. Rare. $100-150.

391. Sebewaing, Sebewaing Brewing Co., 4" chalk, ca. 1955. Rare. $150-225.

392. Seven Eleven, Altes Brewing Co., 12" chalk, ca. 1950s. Rare. $200-300.

393. Simon Pure, William Simon Brewery, 9" molded latex/wood, ca. 1957. $175-250.

394. Southern Select, Galveston-Houston Breweries, 18" chalk, ca. 1935. Rare. $1000+

396. Sterling, Sterling Brewers, 12" chalk, ca. 1960. $250-375.

397. Sterling, Sterling Brewers, 9" chalk, ca. 1960. Music box operates when coin dropped in. $75-100.

395. Standard, Standard Brewing Co., 17" chalk, ca. 1960. $75-100.

398. Sterling, Sterling Brewers, 11.5" chalk, ca. 1960. $100-150.

399. Sterling, Sterling Brewers, 15" metal, ca. 1960. Upon shaking, the bell inside statue gained the bartender's attention for another round. $75-100.

400. Stoney's, Jones Brewing Co., 9.5" chalk, ca. 1948. $350-500.

401. Stoney's, Jones Brewing Co., 8.25" molded latex, ca. 1955. $100-150.

402. Stoney's, Jones Brewing Co., 9.5" molded latex, ca. 1963. $125-175.

403. Stoney's, Jones Brewing Co., 9.5" chalk, ca. 1958. $135-200.

404. Storck, Storck Products Co., 24" paper mache, ca. 1935. Rare. $500-750.

405. Stroh's, Stroh Brewing Co., 8.75" chalk, ca. 1950s. Rare example from the Stroh's achieves. $1000+.

406. Stroh's, Stroh Brewing Co., 7.75" chalk, ca. 1950s. Rare example from the Stroh's achieves. $1000+.

407. Stroh's, Stroh Brewing Co., 10" metal, ca. 1960. Driver's award for meritorious service. $125-175.

408. Stroh's, Stroh Brewing Co., 16" metal/ wood, ca. 1970. Rare. $200-300.

409. Tam O'Shanter, American Brewing Co., 10.5" chalk, ca. 1945. $125-175.

412. Topper, Rochester Brewing Co., 9" chalk, ca. 1940. $75-100.

Topper tray.

410. Tivoli, Tivoli Brewing Co., 16" chalk, ca. 1955. $75-100.

411. Toby Ale, Pilsener Brewing Co., 14" chalk, ca 1940. Rare. $150-225.

413. Tru-Age, Standard Brewing Co., 14.5" chalk, ca. 1946. Rare. $350-500.

414. Utica Club, West End Brewing Co., 9.5" chalk, ca. 1950. Figure known as "Uncle Charlie." $225-325.

415. Utica Club, West End Brewing Co., 9.5" chalk, ca. 1950. Figure known as "Uncle Charlie." $225-325.

Tru-Age tray.

416. Utica Club, West End Brewing Co., 9.5" chalk, ca. 1950. Figure known as "Uncle Charlie." $150-225.

417. Utica Club, West End Brewing Co., 7.5" chalk, ca. 1940. $75-100.

419. Van Merritt, Burlington Brewing Co., 14" chalk, ca. 1950. Rare. $1000+.
419a. Van Merritt, Burlington Brewing Co., 14" chalk, ca. 1950. A rare lighted/motorized version exists. $1000+. Not shown.

418. Valley Forge, Adam Scheidt Brewing Co., 9" metal FSH, ca. 1950. $50-75.

420. Vienna, Vienna Brewing Co., 6.25" chalk ashtray, ca. 1933-40. $30-45.

Valley Forge tray.

421. Vienna, Vienna Brewing Co., 5" composition, ca. 1940. $30-45.

424. Wehle, Wehle Brewing Co., 14.5" chalk, ca. 1933-41. $150-225.

422. Wehle, Wehle Brewing Co., 9.5" chalk, ca. 1933-41. $350-500.

423. Wehle, Wehle Brewing Co., 11.25" chalk, ca. 1933-41. $350-500.

425. West Virginia, Fesenmeier Brewing Co., 10.5" chalk, ca. 1969. $150-225.
425a. West Virginia, Fesenmeier Brewing Co., 10.5" chalk, 1969. Also came with a can. $150-225. Not shown.
425b. West Virginia, Fesenmeier Brewing Co., 10.5" chalk, 1969. Also came with a Christmas tree. $150-225. Not shown.

426. West Virginia, Fesenmeier Brewing Co., 13" chalk, ca. 1969. $250-375.

427. Wielands, John, Pacific Malting and Brewing Co., 9" chalk, ca. 1950. $50-75.

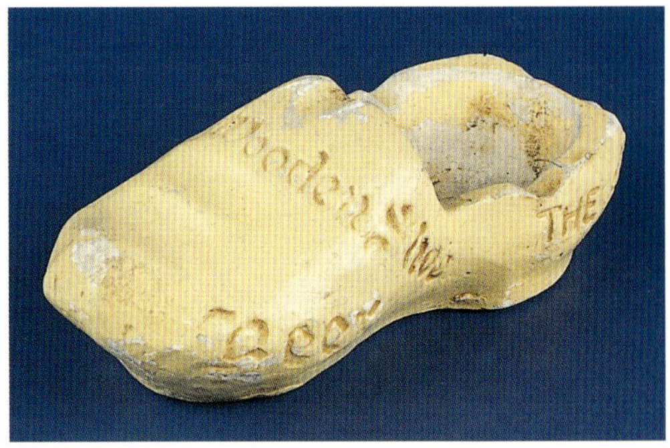

428. Wooden Shoe, Wooden Shoe Brewing Co., 2" chalk ashtray, ca. 1950. $15-25/pair.

429. Wunderbar, Minneapolis Brewing Co., 16" chalk, ca. 1960. $75-100.

430. Wunderbrau, Wunderbrau Brewing Co., 10" chalk, ca. 1951-56. Rare. $1000+.

431. Yankee, Yankee Brewing Co., 12.5" chalk, rare, ca. 1957. Rare. $500-750.

432. Yoerg's, Yoerg Brewing Co., 16" chalk, ca. 1945. Lights. Rare. $500-750.

Chapter Four: Off the Shelf

Small shelf signs, referred to as Shelf Talkers or Misers, are highly collectible items that were used by the makers of more than fifty different brands of beer. The premier company manufacturing Shelf Talkers was Kolograph, of Los Angeles, California. Many of the Shelf Talkers and Misers also included symbols or themes common to the brewery. While the chalk shelf signs from Kolograph are perhaps the most collectible, other similar designs fabricated of plastic, wood, and metal are highly desirable as well. These small signs take up a minimum amount of space and can be easily displayed in a limited display area.

This chapter is divided into two parts. The first part provides a compilation of all known small chalks, mostly from Kolograph. The second part contains many non-chalk Talkers and Misers made of various materials. It provides a first look at many interesting small signs, and serves as the basis for a future project.

Chalk

433. Acme, Acme Breweries, 3" chalk, ca. 1940. $125-175.

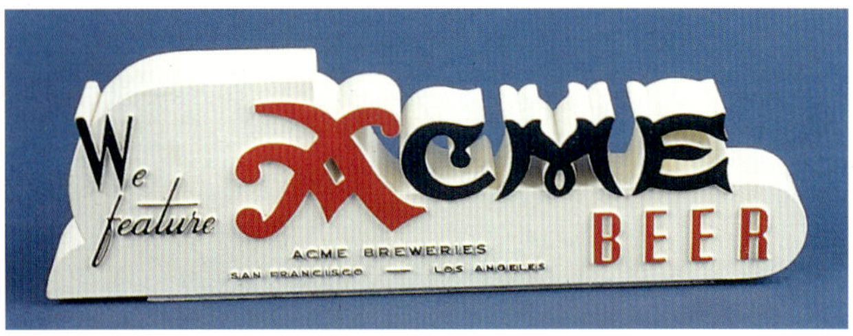

434. Acme, Acme Breweries, 3" chalk, ca. 1940. $175-225.

435. American, American Brewery, 3" chalk, ca. 1958. $175-225.

436. Arrow, Globe Brewing Co., 3" chalk, ca. 1953. $175-225.

437. Bavarian's, Bavarian Brewing Co., 3" chalk, ca. 1953. $125-175.

438. Blitz Weinhard, Blitz-Weinhard Co., 4" chalk, ca. 1950. $175-225.

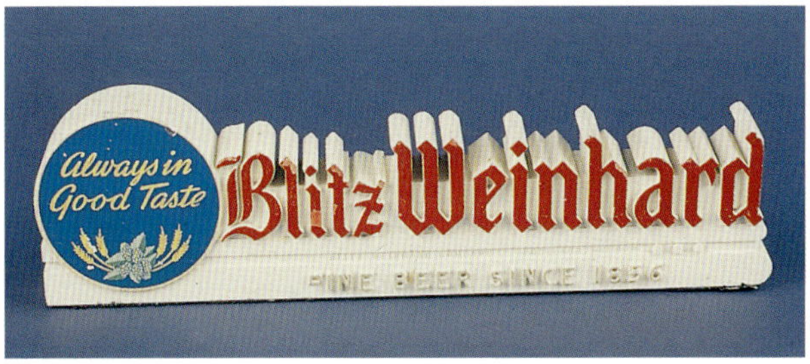

439. Blitz Weinhard, Blitz-Weinhard Co., 3" chalk, ca. 1950. $175-225.

440. Blitz Weinhard, Blitz-Weinhard Co., 3" chalk, ca. 1950. $175-225.

441. Blue 'N Gold, North Bay Brewing Co., 5" chalk, ca. 1955. $75-125.

442. Boh, Enterprise Brewing Co., 5" chalk, ca. 1955. Includes a thermometer. $125-175.

443. Boston Light Ale, Boston Beer Co., 3" chalk, ca. 1940. Rare. $275+.

444. Brew 102, Maier Brewing Co., 5.5" chalk, ca. 1956. Rare. $275+.

445. Burkhardt's, Burkhardt Brewing Co., 3" chalk, ca. 1953. $125-175.

446. Canadian Ace, Canadian Ace Brewing Co., 6" chalk, ca. 1955. $150-200.

447. Champagne Velvet, Terre Haute Brewing Co., 3" chalk, ca. 1952. $125-175.

448. Chief Oshkosh, Oshkosh Brewing Co., 7" chalk, ca. 1950, $175-225.

449. Chief Oshkosh, Oshkosh Brewing Co., 7" chalk, ca. 1950. $175-225.

450. Columbia, Columbia Breweries, 3" chalk, ca. 1950. $75-125.

451. Columbia, Columbia Breweries, 3" chalk, ca. 1948. $175-225.

452. Coor's, Adolph Coors Co., 3" chalk, ca. 1950. $225-275.

453. Diamond State, Diamond State Brewery, 3.5" chalk, ca. 1953-58. Rare. $275+.

454. Drewrys, Drewrys Ltd. USA, 3" chalk, ca. 1947. $125-175.

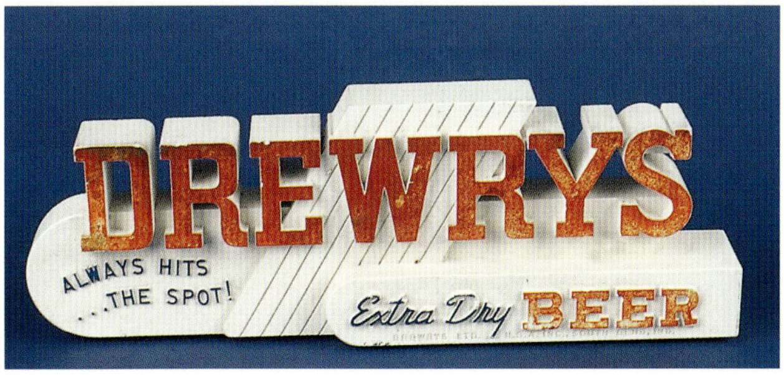

455. Drewrys, Drewrys Ltd. USA, 3" chalk, ca. 1947. $125-175.

456. Drewrys, Drewrys Ltd. USA, 3" chalk, ca. 1947. $125-175.

457. Drewrys, Drewrys Ltd. USA, 3" chalk, ca. 1947. $125-175.

458. E & B, E & B Brewing Co., 4" chalk, ca. 1950.
$175-225.

459. E & B, E & B Brewing Co., 7" chalk, ca. 1950.
$125-175.

460. Eastside, Los Angeles Brewing Co., 4" chalk, ca. 1950.
$125-175.

461. Esquire, Jones Brewing Co., 3" chalk, ca. 1952.
$125-175.

462. Fehr's, Frank Fehr Brewing Co., 3" chalk, ca. 1946.
$125-175.

463. Goebel, Goebel Brewing Co., 4.5" chalk, ca. 1960. $75-125.

464. Goebel, Goebel Brewing Co., 3" chalk, ca. 1960. $75-125.

465. Goebel, Goebel Brewing Co., 5" chalk, ca. 1960. $125-175.

466. Gretz, Wm. Gretz Brewing Co., 3" chalk, ca. 1958. $125-175.

Gretz tray.

467. Hanley, James Hanley Co., 3" chalk, ca. 1950. Rare. $275+.

468. Iron City, Pittsburgh Brewing Co., 3" chalk, ca. 1950. $225-275.

469. Jung's, Wm. G. Jung Brewing Co., 3.5" chalk, ca. 1950s. Rare. $275+.

473. Lemp, Wm. J. Lemp Brewing Co., 4" chalk, ca. 1940. $175-225.

470. Kamm's, Kamm & Schellinger Co., 3" chalk, ca. 1955. $175-225.

474. Lucky Lager, Lucky Lager Brewing Co., 3.25" chalk, ca. 1950. $125-175.

475. Luxury, Los Angeles Brewing Co., 4" chalk, ca. 1948. $175-225.

471. Koehler's, Erie Brewing Co., 6" chalk, ca. 1955. $125-175.

476. National Bohemian, National Brewing Co., 3" chalk, ca. 1950. Rare. $275+.

472. Koehler's, Erie Brewing Co., 5.5" chalk, ca. 1955. $125-175.

477. Old Dutch, Eagle Brewing Co., 3" chalk, ca. 1952. $125-175.

478. Old Export, Cumberland Brewing Co., 3" chalk, ca. 1950. $125-175.

479. P.O.C., Pilsener Brewing Co., 5" chalk, ca. 1955. $125-175.

480. Pennsylvania Dutch, Lebanon Valley Brewing Co., 3" chalk, ca. 1952-58. $125-175.

481. Rainier, Sicks Rainier Brewing Co., 4" chalk, ca. 1940. $275+.

482. Rainier, Sicks Rainier Brewing Co., 4" chalk, ca. 1940. Rare. $175-225.

483. Schmidt's, Schmidt Brewing Co., 4" chalk, ca. 1960. Rare. $275+.

484. Sicks' Select, Sicks Brewing Co., 4" chalk, ca. 1955. $175-225.

485. Silver Top, Duquesne Brewing Co., 4" chalk, ca. 1960. $125-175.

486. Standard, Standard Brewing Co., 3" chalk, ca. 1946. $125-175.

487. Stoney's, Jones Brewing Co., 6" chalk, ca. 1950. $125-175.

488. Weber, Weber Waukesha Brewing Co., 3" chalk, ca. 1946. $175-225.

489. Weber, Weber Waukesha Brewing Co., 5" chalk, ca. 1950. $125-175.

490. Wooden Shoe, Wooden Shoe Brewing Co., 6" chalk, ca. 1945. $175-225.

491. Wooden Shoe, Wooden Shoe Brewing Co., 6" chalk, ca. 1945. $175-225.

492. Wooden Shoe, Wooden Shoe Brewing Co., 6" chalk, ca. 1945. Rare. $175-225.

Other Materials

493. Altes, Altes Brewing Co., 7" composite, ca. 1945. $30-45.

495. Arrow 77, Globe Brewing Co., 9" plastic, ca. 1960. $10-15.

494. American, American Brewery, 8.5" composition, ca. 1956. Similar to Gettelman #515. $50-75.

496. Berghoff, Berghoff Brewing Co., 3.25" plastic, ca. 1956. $15-25.

497. Brewers Best, Grace Bros. Brewing Co., 4" metal/paper, ca. 1960. $25-35.

498. Burger, Burger Brewing Co., 3" metal/composition, ca. 1950. $35-50.

499. Burger, Burger Brewing Co., 4" composition, ca. 1950. $35-50.

503. Drewrys, Drewrys Ltd. USA, 3" wood, ca. 1947. $75-100.

500. Champagne Velvet, Terre Haute Brewing Co., 3" aluminium, ca. 1952. $60-90.

504. Drewrys, Drewrys Ltd. USA, 4.5" plastic, ca. 1960. $15-25.

501. City Club, Jacob Schmidt Brewing Co., 3" wood, ca. 1951. $75-100.

505. Drewrys, Drewrys Ltd. USA, 4.5" plastic, ca. 1960. $15-25.

502. Drewrys, Drewrys Ltd. USA, 4.5" wood, ca. 1947. $75-100.

506. Drewrys, Drewrys Ltd. USA, 5" plastic, ca. 1960. $15-25.

507. Duquesne, Duquesne Brewing Co., 7.5" wood/plastic, ca. 1955. $15-25.

508. E & B, E & B Brewing Co., 6" wood, ca. 1958. $35-50.

509. Falstaff, Falstaff Brewing Co., 8.5" wood, ca. 1955. $15-25.

510. Frankenmuth, Frankenmuth Brewing Co., 4" wood, ca. 1955. $20-30.

511. Frankenmuth, Frankenmuth Brewing Co., 4" plastic, ca. 1950. $25-40.

512. Frankenmuth, Frankenmuth Brewing Co., 4" plastic, ca. 1950. $25-40.

513. Friars, Friars Ale Brewing Co., 5" wood, ca. 1956. $50-75.

514. Gettelman, A. Gettelman Brewing Co., 6.5" wood, ca. 1950. $50-75.

515. Gettelman, A. Gettelman Brewing Co., 8.5" composition, Similar to American #494, ca. 1956. $50-75.

516. Goebel, Goebel Brewing Co., 4.5" plastic, ca. 1953. $20-30.

517. Goebel, Goebel Brewing Co., 6" plastic, ca. 1960. $10-15.

518. Grain belt, Minneapolis Brewing Co., 10.5" plastic, ca. 1965. $10-15.

519. Gunther's, Gunther Brewing Co., 3" plastic, ca. 1950s, $25-40.

520. Hanley's, James Hanley Co., 4" plastic, ca. 1930s. $60-90.

523. Hohenadel, John Hohenadel Brewery, 7" composition, ca. 1946. $125-175.

521. Heidelberg, Heidelberg Brewing Co., 6" composition, ca. 1955. $30-45.

522. Heidelberg, Heidelberg Brewing Co., 3.5" wood, ca. 1955. $40-60.

524. Hull's, Hull Brewing Co., 9" composition, 1950. $30-45.

525. Hyde Park, Hyde Park Brewing Assn., 5"metal/paper, ca. 1950. $50-75.

526. Kingsbury, Kingsbury Breweries, 5" plastic/wood, ca. 1950. $35-50.

528. Miller, Miller Brewing Co., 8" plastic, ca. 1950. $20-30.

527. Lucky Lager, Lucky Lager Brewing Co., 4" metal/paper, 1960. $25-35.

529. Miller, Miller Brewing Co., 6" plastic, ca. 1950. $40-60.

530. Old Style, G. Heileman Brewing Co., 4" composition, ca. 1955. $20-30.

532. Pfeiffer's, Pfeiffer Brewing Co., 4" plastic, ca. 1954. $20-30.

531. Pabst, Pabst Brewing Co., 9" plastic, ca. 1950. $35-50.

533. Rheingold, Liebmann Breweries, 8.5" plastic, ca. 1960. $20-30.

534. Rolling Rock, Latrobe Brewing Co., 3" plastic, ca. 1960. $10-15.

535. Rolling Rock, Latrobe Brewing Co., 8" plastic/wood, ca. 1950. $15-25.

536. Schmidt's, C. Schmidt & Sons, 8.5" plastic, ca. 1950. $60-90.

537. Schoenling, Schoenling Brewing Co., 4" plastic, ca. 1965. $15-25.

538. Sicks' Select, Sicks Brewing Co., 8" plastic, ca. 1950. $30-45.

539. Stag, Griesedieck-Western Brewery Co., 4" plastic, ca. 1950. $15-25.

540. Valley Brew, El Dorado Brewing Co., 4.25" plastic, ca. 1950. $15-25.

Chapter Five: Waiting For a Live One!

Employing the perfect setting to market their products, several breweries captured the moment by depicting male customers and/or bartenders gathered around the bar enjoying a cold one. This same theme is often seen in a wall hanging called "Waiting for a Live One," rarely found advertising a brand of beer, but shown here as a plaque from Garden City Brewing of Chicago in Figure 11.

Figure 11. Garden City Brewing plaque.

Identical or very similar back bar statues were used by at least eight different brewery brands. The American (541) and Burkhardt's (542) are identical except for the brand name. Similarly, the barbershop quartets depicted in Iron City (545), Regal (547), and Tech (548) are identical, as are the Heidelberg (544) and Yusay's (549 and 551). The Heidelberg bar scenes came in a lighted (544) and a non-lighted (544a) version. The purpose of the two tiny screws found at the top edge of many Heidelberg bar scenes was to hold the light in place. A similar design to the Yusay's is the Gibbons (543), which, while close in design, is slightly wider.

It is important to note that none of the cream-colored statues shown came as a full-color painted version, other than the Yusay 550. Persons often try to promote painted versions of the cream colored bar scenes as authentic. Only the full-color version of the bar scenes included a real glass mirror behind the bartender; none of the cream versions had a real mirror. Additionally, only the painted versions included a sign to the right of the bartender announcing "a boxing match tonight."

542. Burkhardt's, Burkhardt Brewing Co., 9" chalk, ca. 1953. $100-150.

541. American, American Brewery, 9.5" chalk, ca. 1958. $150-225.

543. Gibbons, The Lion Inc., 9" chalk, ca. 1946. $75-100.

544. Heidelberg, Heidelberg Brewing Co., 11" chalk, ca. 1955. Lighted version. $75-100.
544a. Heidelberg, Heidelberg Brewing Co., 9" chalk, ca. 1955. Non-lighted version. $75-100. Not shown.

546. Iron City, Pittsburgh Brewing Co., 10" chalk, ca. 1958. $75-100.

545. Iron City, Pittsburgh Brewing Co., 10" chalk, ca. 1958. $75-100.

Below:
547. Regal Pale, Regal Pale Brewing Co., 10" chalk, ca. 1956. $150-225.

548. Tech, Pittsburgh Brewing Co., 10" chalk, ca. 1950. $100-150.

Yusay tray.

550. Yusay, Pilsen Brewing Co., 9" chalk, ca. 1950. $125-175.

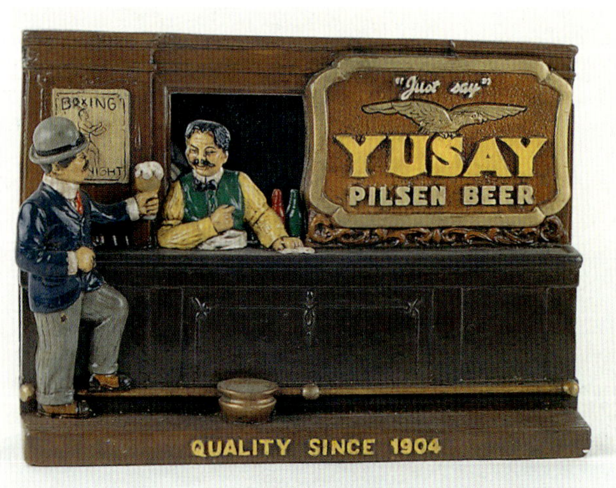

549. Yu say, Pilsen Brewing Co., 9" chalk, ca. 1950. $100-150.

551. Yusay, Pilsen Brewing Co., 9" chalk, ca. 1950. $100-150.

Chapter Six: Got to Hand It to You

More than twenty breweries used a hand grasping a beer bottle to market their product. An extremely rare salesman's sample of a generic hand is shown as statue 552.

552. Generic salesman's hand, 14" (with bottle) chalk right hand, ca. 1955. Rare. $100-150.

553. Altes, Altes Brewing Co., 14" chalk right hand, ca. 1953. $75-100.
553a. Altes, Altes Brewing Co., 14" chalk right hand, ca. 1953. Also made holding can. $75-100. Not shown.

Every beer brand known that featured a hand employed a right hand. Some brands also featured a left. No brands have been noted where only a left hand exists. The size of the opening in the hand permitted only a bottle to be held, except for Altes (553 and 554) and Oertel's (572 and 573), which can hold either a 12-ounce can or a bottle. It is not clear whether cans were ever intended to be displayed in these statues or if they fit only because the opening is slightly oversize.

The only hand made in a lighted version was the Leinenkugel's (568), which holds a plastic bottle. Two brands, the rare Fort Pitt (560) and Kamm's (564), display a hand holding a glass of beer next to a bottle. While women were generally not included in beer advertising, the Fehr's (559), Lone Star (569), and West Virginia (588) depicted a gloved hand, lovingly holding a bottle of the respective brew. Hands usually held only 12-ounce bottles, except for the Schoenling (581) that held a quart bottle. This Schoenling hand was used in package goods stores, as it is unlikely quarts were being marketed in bars. As with barrels (see next Chapter), the hand statue appears to be primarily an American phenomenon.

554. Altes, Altes Brewing Co., 14" chalk left hand, ca. 1953. $75-100.
554a. Altes, Altes Brewing Co., 14" chalk left hand, ca. 1953. Also made holding can. $75-100. Not shown.

555. Brew 77, Wm. Gerst Brewing Co., 14" chalk right hand, ca. 1949-51. Rare. $150-225.

556. Brew 102, Maier Brewing Co., 14" chalk right hand, ca. 1956. Rare. $150-225.

557. Dakota, Dakota Malting & Brewing Co., 15" chalk right hand, ca. 1933-47. Rare. $150-225.

558. Diplomat, Cremo Brewing Co., 14" chalk right hand, ca. 1949-55. Rare. $150-225.

559. Fehr's, Frank Fehr Brewing Co., 15.5" chalk woman's right hand, ca. 1952. $150-225.

560. Fort Pitt, Fort Pitt Brewing Co., 11", chalk right hand, ca. 1938. Rare. $150-225.

561. Fort Pitt, Fort Pitt Brewing Co., 13" chalk right hand, ca. 1965. $50-75.

563. Hanley Export, James Hanley Co., 12.5" chalk right hand, ca. 1955. $75-100.

562. Gold Label, California Brewing Co., 14" chalk right hand, ca. 1955. $100-150.

564. Kamm's, Kamm & Schellinger Co., 11" chalk right hand, ca. 1950. $150-225.

565. Leinekugel's, Jacob Leinenkugel Brewing Co., 14" chalk left hand, ca. 1950. $75-100.
566. Leinekugel's, Jacob Leinenkugel Brewing Co., 14" chalk right hand, ca. 1950. $75-100.

569. Lone Star, Lone Star Brewing Co., 16" chalk, ca. 1950. Rare. $200-300.

567. Leinekugel's, Jacob Leinenkugel Brewing Co., 13.5" plastic right hand, ca. 1980. $40-60.

568. Leinekugel's, Jacob Leinenkugel Brewing Co., 15" plastic lighted right hand, ca. 1990. $35-50.

570. National Bohemian, National Brewing Co., 14" chalk, right hand, ca. 1958. Rare. $150-225.

571. Oertels, Oertel Brewing Co., 14" chalk right hand, ca. 1939. This is the original Oertels hand with the correct Oertels stubby bottle. Rare. $200-300.

574. Old Export, Cumberland Brewing Co., 14" chalk right hand, ca. 1950. $125-175.

575. Renner, Renner Co., 14" chalk right hand, ca. 1946. Rare. $150-225.

572. Oertels, Oertel Brewing Co., 9" chalk left hand, ca. 1954. This is an authentic Oertels hand. It was produced commercially. Rare. $150-225.

573. Oertels, Oertel Brewing Co., 9" chalk right hand, ca. 1954. Also available holding a bottle. This hand is being reproduced. $150-225 for rare authentic version, $25-40 for the reproduction.

576. Rheingold, United States Brewing Co., 14" (with bottle) chalk right hand, ca. 1946. Rare. $125-175.

577. Royal Bohemian, Duluth Brewing and Malting Co., 14" chalk left hand, ca. 1955. $75-100.
578. Royal Bohemian, Duluth Brewing and Malting Co., 14" chalk right hand, ca. 1955. $75-100.

581. Schoenling, Schoenling Brewing Co., 16" chalk right hand holding quart bottle, ca. 1950. $150-225.

579. Schoenling, Schoenling Brewing Co., 14" chalk left hand, ca. 1950. $75-100.
580. Schoenling, Schoenling Brewing Co., 14" chalk right hand, ca. 1950. $75-100.

582. Stern Brau, Star Peerless Brewing, 14" chalk right hand, ca. 1946. Rare.$100-150.

583. Tadcaster, Worcester Brewing Co., 14" chalk right hand, ca. 1960. Rare. $150-225.

584. Valley Forge, Adam Scheidt Brewing Co., 14" chalk left hand, ca. 1950. $60-90.
585. Valley Forge, Adam Scheidt Brewing Co., 14" chalk right hand, ca. 1950. $60-90.

587. Van Merritt, Burlington Brewing Co., 14" chalk right hand, ca. 1960. $125-175.

586. Van Merritt, Burlington Brewing Co., 14" chalk right hand, ca. 1960. $150-225.

588. West Virginia, Fesenmeier Brewing Co., 15" chalk woman's right hand, ca. 1965. $200-300.

Chapter Seven: Roll Out the Barrel

What better way to promote a beer theme than with barrels of beer! The universal method of bulk beer storage, the barrel, served not only as a bank for many brands, but also as the holder of foam scrapers for Lion (610) and Krueger (608). The Tivoli barrel (631) served as a cigar tip cutter. The use of barrels as a POP item appears to have been essentially an American theme, as very few foreign barrel banks are known. Barrel banks were often placed on the bar to encourage patrons to insert their spare change as tips for the bartender!

While most barrels were chalk, a few plastic and wood ones were made. Chalk barrels were fortunate to survive frequent quests for "saved coins." The bank barrels were usually 6.5", 8", or 12.5" in height. The Blatz (27 and 28) barrels in Chapter Three came only with the Blatz man sitting on the top. Sometimes they are sold incorrectly with the Blatz man missing. A rare lamp version of the Blatz (28) barrel (shown as 29 in Chapter Three) still has the original barrel lamp globe. Ceramic barrels from Metz and My were made by McCoy, a well-known pottery company. The majority of barrels were three dimensional; however, several brands like Bavarians (589), Goebel 22 (604), Hudepohl (606), Ortlieb's (623), and Wehle (632) made "half" barrels intended for setting on a back bar. Freestanding barrel ends were used as shelf signs by some breweries, including the rare Hyde Park (212). The DuBois Budweiser (109) barrel end was the target of a potential lawsuit by Anheuser-Busch, which claimed a trademark infringement for the name Budweiser.

589. Bavarian's, Bavarian Brewing Co., 12.5" chalk half barrel, ca. 1953. $50-75.

590. Blatz, Blatz Brewing Co., 8" wood, ca. 1950. $20-30.

591. Brew 66, Sicks Brewing Co., 12.5" chalk, ca. 1950. $60-90.

592. Bruck's, Bruckmann Co., 10" chalk, ca. 1937-49. $150-225.

595. Duquesne, Duquesne Brewing Co., 8" chalk, ca. 1956. $35-50.

593. Chief Oshkosh, Oshkosh Brewing Co., 8" chalk, ca. 1957. $40-60.

596. Duquesne, Duquesne Brewing Co., 12" wood, ca. 1947. $50-75.

594. Chief Oshkosh, Oshkosh Brewing Co., 8" chalk/wood, ca. 1957. Barrel and glass display. $80-120.

597. Erin Brew, Standard Brewing Co., 8" chalk, ca. 1952. $35-50.

598. Erin Brew, Standard Brewing Co., 8" chalk, ca. 1958. $35-50.

600. Erin Brew, Standard Brewing Co., 12.5" chalk, ca. 1952. $50-75.

599. Erin Brew, Standard Brewing Co., 8" chalk, ca. 1952. $35-50.

602. Fitgers, Fitgers Brewing Co., 8" chalk, ca. 1965. $50-75.

601. Erin Brew, Standard Brewing Co., 12.5" chalk, ca. 1950. $50-75.

603. Genesee, Genesee Brewing Co., 12" Styrofoam half barrel, ca. 1960s. $10-15.

604. Goebel, Goebel Brewing Co., 12" chalk half barrel, ca. 1953. $35-50.

605. Hamm's, Theo Hamm's Brewing Co., 5.5" wood, ca. 1970. Krüg Klub, a gift to distributors. $25-40.

606. Hudepohl, Hudepohl Brewing Co., 12" chalk half barrel, ca. 1960. $50-75.

608. Krueger, G. Krueger Brewing Co., 7" molded latex FSH, ca. 1936. $50-75.

607. Koch's, Fred Koch Brewery, 8" chalk, ca. 1955. $35-50.

609. Krueger, G. Krueger Brewing Co., 7" metal FSH, ca. 1936. $50-75.

610. Lion, Lion Brewery of New York City, 7" wood FSH, ca. 1945. $25-40.

611. Lone Star, Lone Star Brewing Co., 8" chalk, ca. 1960. $40-60.

612. Meister Brau, Meister Brau Brewing Co., 8" chalk, ca. 1946. $40-60.
612a. Meister Brau, Meister Brau Brewing Co., 12.5" chalk, ca. 1946. $60-90. Not shown.

613. Metz, Metz Brewing Co., 8" chalk, ca. 1950. $40-60.
613a. Metz, Metz Brewing Co., 12" chalk, ca. 1950. Same wording as 8" barrel. $50-75. Not shown.

614. Metz, Metz Brewing Co., 8" ceramic left side, ca. 1950. $40-60.
615. Metz, Metz Brewing Co., 6.5" ceramic right side, ca. 1950. $25-40.

Right:
618. Metz, Metz Brewing Co., 8" ceramic, ca. 1950. $40-60.

616. Metz, Metz Brewing Co., 6.5" ceramic, ca. 1950. $25-40.

619. My, My Brewing Co., 6.5" ceramic, ca. 1950. $60-90.

621. Neuweiler, Louis F. Neuweiler's & Sons, 8" chalk, ca. 1955. $40-60.

617. Metz, Metz Brewing Co., 6.5" ceramic, ca. 1950. $25-40.

620. National Bohemian, National Brewing Co., 7" chalk, ca. 1950. $100-150.

622. Oertels, Oertel Brewing Co., 12.5" chalk, ca. 1950. $50-75.

624. Peter Hand's, Peter Hand Brewery, 8" chalk, ca. 1955. $40-60.
624a. Peter Hand's, Peter Hand Brewery, 12.5" chalk, ca. 1955. Same wording as 8" barrel. $50-75. Not shown.

626. Rainier, Sicks Rainier Brewing Co., 7" chalk, ca. 1956. $60-90.

623. Ortliebs, Henry F. Ortlieb Brewing Co., 12" chalk half barrel, ca. 1963. $35-50.

625. Piels, Piels Bros., 7" plastic, ca. 1970. $10-20.

Below:
627. Schell's, August Schell Brewing Co., 9" chalk, ca. 1960. $75-100.

630. Tivoli, Tivoli Brewing Co., 8" chalk, ca. 1955. $40-60.
630a. Tivoli, Tivoli Brewing Co., 12.5" chalk, ca. 1955. Same wording as 8" barrel. $50-75. Not shown.

632. Wehle, Wehle Brewing Co., 14" chalk half barrel, ca. 1933-41. $250-300.

628. Standard, Standard Brewing Co., 12.5" chalk, ca. 1960. $50-75.

631. Tivoli, Tivoli Brewing Co., 7" wood cigar cutter, ca. 1890s. Rare. $300-450.

629. Standard, Standard Brewing Co., 12.5" chalk, ca. 1960. $60-90.

633. West Virginia, Fesenmeier Brewing Co., 8" chalk, ca. 1965. $50-75.

Chapter Eight: Odds 'N' Ends

Miniature Bottle Statues

Five different generic figurines commonly used to hold miniature beer bottles are often included in back bar collections. Fill's Specialty Manufacturing Company of Milwaukee, Wisconsin produced these from 1950 to 1955. Figures 634 to 637 show four of the common ones. Bartender Joe (634) is the most common, followed by the black base Lucky Guy fisherman (635), the Set 'Em Up bowling pin (637) and, the rarest of the group, the white base Lucky Guy fisherman (636). The plastic fisherman (638) is also reasonably difficult to find. Dozens of beer brands were marketed using these figures, which were sold to souvenir shops and brewery gift stores. Since hundreds of beers were labeled as mini-bottles, it is not possible to verify the authenticity of most combinations beyond common brands like Budweiser, Blatz, Drewry, Gettelman, Pabst, and Old Export. Collectors should be aware of offers touting these generic-type statues with unusual or rare bottles. Only Drewrys (see Figure 13) employed miniature bottles in their commercial statues' marketing plan.

636. Lucky Guy-Style 2 Fisherman, 7" polymer resin, ca. 1950-1955, $40-60.

637. Set Em Up-Bowling Pin, 7" polymer resin, ca. 1950-1955, $40-60.

634. Bartender Joe, 7" polymer resin, ca. 1950-1955, $25-40.

635. Lucky Guy-Style 1 Fisherman, 7" polymer resin, ca. 1950-1955, $30-45.

638. Worth Fishing For!, 6.5" plastic, ca. 1960, $30-45.

Below:
Figure 13. Drewry' s Miniature Bottle Statues.

Please Pass the Salt and Pepper

Figural salt and pepper shakers are interesting go-withs that do not take up much space, can be gathered at a reasonable cost, and deliver their contents if desired.

639. Griesedieck, Griesedieck Bros. Brewing Co., 3" wood salt and pepper shakers, ca. 1940. $50-75/pair.

640. Hamm's, Theo Hamm's Brewing Co., 4" ceramic salt and pepper shakers, ca. 1965. $100-150/pair.

641. Peerless, Lacrosse Breweries, 5" plastic salt and pepper shakers, ca. 1940. $30-45/pair.

642. Piels, Piel Bros., 4" ceramic salt and pepper shakers, ca. 1960. $100-150/pair.

Ashes to Ashes

Small ashtrays are another go-with requiring little space and, like the salt and peppers, offering a second function, if needed around the bar. Several of these were also shown in Chapter Three, but are illustrated again here to show the variety of ashtrays available.

643. Chief Oshkosh, Oshkosh Brewing Co., 2" chalk ashtray, ca. 1946. $25-40.

644. Coor's, Novelty, 6" chalk novelty ashtray, ca. 1970. $10-20.

105. Drewrys, Drewrys Ltd. USA, 7" chalk ashtray, ca. 1947. Rare. $100-150.

645. Haefner's, Haefner Brewing Co., 5" metal ashtray, ca. 1940, $25-35.

647. Old Style, G. Heilman Brewing Co., 7.5" metal ashtray, ca. 1950. $35-50.

420. Vienna, Vienna Brewing Co., 6.25" chalk ashtray, ca. 1933-40. $30-45.

646. Hamm's, Theo Hamm's Brewing Co., 1.5" ceramic ashtray, ca. 1960. $50-75.

648. Standard, Standard Brewing Co., 3.5" chalk ashtray, ca. 1945. $20-30.

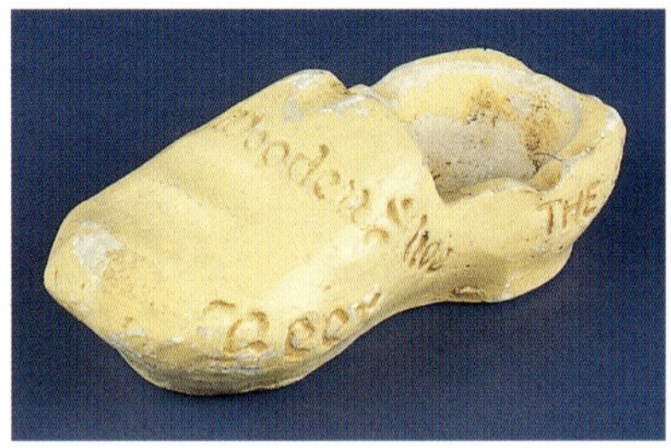

428. Wooden Shoe, Wooden Shoe Brewing Co., 2" chalk ashtray, ca. 1950. $15-25/pair.

Fakes and Novelties Mistaken for Beer Statues

The Oertel's ashtray (662) and hands (660-661) were previously disclosed as fakes. Similarly, the Oertel's man (264) *was* authentic, but reproductions have been made. Refer to Chapters Three and Six for more detail. The Pitt's Ale (665) is a repaint of a non-beer statue. Two other of the more common non-beer items are the Falstaff (649) and Pickwick (664) men that are actually novelties. Neither was issued by a brewery, yet they are often touted as such by sellers. The Schlitz Malt Liquor (666) is as near perfect a fake as any non-beer conversion seen.

649. Falstaff, Novelty, 5.5" chalk, ca. 1960. Novelty, not issued by brewery. These were made in numerous colors. $5-10.

650. Lone Star, Novelty, 12.5" chalk, ca. 1980. $75-100.

652. Lone Star, Novelty, 7.5" chalk, ca. 1980. $15-25.

653. Lone Star, Novelty, 6.5" chalk, ca. 1980. $15-25.

651. Lone Star, Novelty, 14" chalk, ca. 1980. $75-100.

654. Lone Star, Novelty, 8" chalk, ca. 1990. $15-25.

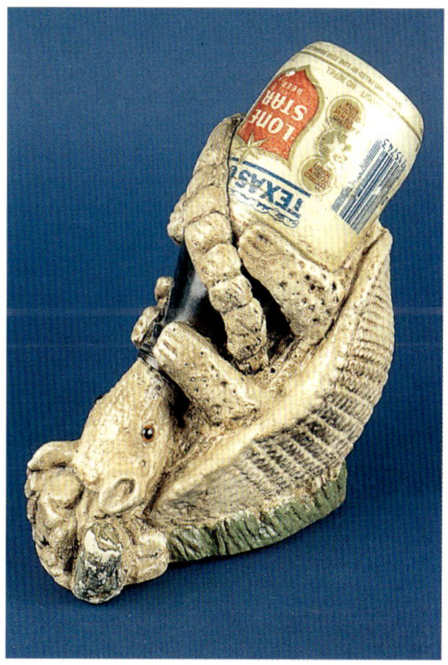

655. Lone Star, Novelty, 7.5" chalk, ca. 1980. $15-25.

656. Lone Star, Novelty, 8" chalk, ca. 1980. $15-25.

660. Oertels, not authentic, 14" chalk right hand painted black, ca. 1990s. $25-40 for reproduction.

661. Oertels, not authentic, 9.75" chalk right hand, ca. 1939 for original statue. This hand originally held the stubby bottle shown in statue #571, not a Crowntainer. The hand shown is a fake. $25-40 for fake.

657. Lone Star, Novelty, 7.5" chalk (right), ca. 1980. $10-15.
658. Lone Star, Novelty, 7.5" chalk (center), ca. 1980. $10-15.
659. Lone Star, Novelty, 7.5" chalk (left), ca. 1980. $10-15.

662. Oertels, Novelty, 7.75" chalk ashtray. This statue is a fake and was made from the base of statue #264, the Oertels man. $25-40.

663. Pabst, Fake, 10" chalk, 1991s. This statue is an absolute fake. $50-75.

Right:
665. Pitt's, Novelty, 14" chalk, ca. unknown. This is a fake statue. The Pitt's brand name never existed. $50-75.

664. Pickwick, Novelty, 8" chalk, ca. Unknown. This is not a beer statue issued by the Pickwick Brewery. $25-40.

666. Schlitz, Fake, 9" ceramic, ca. unknown. This is a fake statue. $10-20.

Circle the Wagons

Several breweries used covered wagon themes as POP advertising. Four such examples are shown here for those collectors who consider them in the statue family, as well as an Indian Tepee for good luck.

667. Fisher, General Brewing Co., 8.5" wood/cloth, ca. 1972-78. $75-100.

668. Gold Label, Maier Brewing Co., 10.5" wood/cloth, ca. 1960. $50-75.

669. Olympia, Olympia Brewing Co., 10.5" wood/cloth, ca. 1965. $50-75.

670. Pfeiffer, Pfeiffer Brewing Co., 9" wood/cloth, ca. 1960, $35-50.

671. Schmidt, Associated Brewing Co., 9" wood/cloth, ca. 1965. $40-60.

Little Bartenders

All items shown here are non-branded "go-withs" found behind the bar. One commercial pretzel holder from Pabst (302, also shown in Chapter Three) appears very similar to statues 674 and 675. Statue 673 is a bartender from Bemco, a supplier of sundry items to the tavern industry. The small bartender with three mugs (677) resembles the Vienna figurine (421), but is not identified with a brand name.

672. Schmidt, Associated Brewing Co., 23" wood/cloth, ca. 1965. $75-100.

673. Bemco Bartender, 11" chalk, ca. 1950. $50 75.

674. Pretzel Holder Bartender, 10" chalk, ca. 1950. $10-15.

675. Pretzel Holder Bartender, 10" chalk, ca. 1950. $10-15.

302. Pabst, Pabst Brewing Co., 10" chalk pretzel holder, ca. 1955. $150-225.

676. Free Lunch Novelty Bartender, 10" chalk, ca. 1950. $15-25.

677. Bottle Opener Novelty Bartender, 5" chalk, ca. 1940. Looks like the figurines from Vienna Beer. $10-15

Bibliography

Anderson, Sonja, and Will Anderson. *Beers, Breweries and Breweriana*. Carmel, NY: 1969.

Anderson, Will. *The Beer Book*. Princeton, NJ: Pyne Press, 1973.

Baley, George J. *Back Bar Breweriana*. Gas City, IN: L-W Book Sales, 1994.

Beer Can Collectors of America. *United States Beer Cans*. Fenton, MO: Josten Inc., 2001.

Burden, Paul. *The Beer Tray Book*. Medfield, PA: Norfield Publishing, 1992.

Cameron, Jeffrey C. *The Class Book of U.S. Beer Cans*. Souderton, PA: Class Publishing Company, 1982.

Cornell, Martyn. *Beer Memorabilia*. Edison, NY: Chartwell Books, 2000.

Haydock, Herb, and Helen Haydock. *The World Book of Beer Memorabilia*. Paducah, KY: Turner Publishing, 1997.

Kay, Robert E. *Miniature Beer Bottles & Go-Withs*. Batavia, IL: K & K Publishers, 1980.

Ojala, Reino. *20 Years of American Beers – The '30s & 40s*. Minneapolis, MN: Published by Author, Winslow Printing.

Straub, Gary. *Collectible Beer Trays*. Atglen, PA: Schiffer Publishing Ltd., 1995.

Wieren, Dale P. *American Breweries II*. West Point, PA; Eastern Coast Breweriana Association, 1995.

Vetter, John, *The New WHO's WHO In Brew*. Fairfax, VA; The Pressworks, 2000.

Appendix A: Breweriana Collector Clubs

National Association of Breweriana Advertising (NABA)
John Stanley
P.O. Box 64
Chapel Hill, NC 27514-0064

Beer Can Collectors of America (BCCA)
747 Merus Ct.
Fenton, MO 63026-2092

American Breweriana Association (ABA)
P.O. Box 11157
Pueblo, CO 81001-0157

Eastern Coast Breweriana Association (ECBA)
John Stanley,
P.O. Box 64
Chapel Hill, NC 27514-0064

Appendix B: Statue Manufacturing Companies

The following companies manufactured back bar breweriana represented in this book.

Alexander Corp., Philadelphia, Pennsylvania
Bosograf, E.M., Chicago, Illinois
Central States Specialties Co
Davis, A.O., Coshocton, Ohio
DeepFlex
Effective Advertising, New York, New York
Embossograph Display Mfg. Co, Chicago, Illinois
Florence Art Inc., San Francisco, California
General States Specialty
Gilroy Reproductions
Golden, B.J., Pittsburgh, Pennsylvania
Handicraft (Till Mac), Los Angles, California
Kolorgraph Inc., Louisville, Kentucky
KCS Mfg, Milwaukee, Wisconsin
Louis Composition Products, Detroit, Michigan
Martelle-Lamb Inc., Louisville, Kentucky
Matte Advertising Display, Louisville, Kentucky
Modern Tuscany Art Co., Philadelphia, Pennsylvania
Phase Four Products, New York, New York
Plastic Form Co.
Plasto Manufacturing Company, Chicago, Illinois
Process Displays, Milwaukee, Wisconsin
Schultz, Thomas & Co., Morton Grove, Illinois
Silvestri Bros. Co.
Smith, W.J., Louisville, Kentucky
Tilimne Handicraft,
Timely Products, Des Moines, Iowa

Index

Brewery	City	State	Photo Reference Numbers	In Business
Frankenmuth Brewing Co.	Frankenmuth	MI	144-152, 510-512	1933-54
Fred Koch Brewery	Dunkirk	NY	22, 607	1973-89
Friars Ale Brewing Co.	Port Huron	MI	513	1944-53
G. Heileman Brewing Co.	LaCrosse	WI	197, 291, 530, 647	1937-40
G. Krueger Brewing Co.	Newark	NJ	608-609	1933-60
Galveston-Houston Breweries	Galveston	TX	394	1933-55
Garden City Brewery	Chicago	IL	267	1936-50
General Brewing Corporation	San Francisco	CA	20-21, 235, 667	1933-48
Genesee Brewing Co.	Rochester	NY	603	1934-
Gerst Wm., Brewing Co	Nashville	TN	555	1949-51
Gettlelman, A, Brewing Co.	Milwaukee	WI	153, 514-515	1933-62
Globe Brewing Co.	Baltimore	MD	436, 495	1964-73
Gluek Brewing Co.	Minneapolis	MN	156	1933-65
Goebel Brewing Co.	Detroit	MI	157-161, 463-465, 516-517, 604	1933-58
Golden West Brewing Co.	Oakland	CA	163	1933-40
Grace Bros. Brewing Co	Santa Rosa	CA	81, 497	1956-62
Gretz, Wm., Brewing Co.	Philadelphia	PA	466	1935-60
Griesedieck Bros Brewing Co	St. Louis	MO	166, 539, 639	1933-58
Gulf Brewing Co.	Houston	TX	164-165	1933-63
Gunther Brewing Co.	Baltimore	MD	167-168, 519	1933-59
Haefner Brewing Co.	Lancaster	PA	645	1933-45
Haffenreffer & Co.	Boston	MA	327	1933-62
Hals Brewing Co.	Baltimore	MD	169-171	1954-63
Hamm's, Theo, Brewing Co.	St. Paul	MN	172-184, 605, 640, 646	1933-75
Hampden Brewing Co.	Willimansett	MA	185	1937-57
Hand, Peter, Brewery	Chicago	IL	624	1933-88
Hanley, James, Co.	Providence	RI	186-189, 467, 520, 563	1933-51
Heidelberg Brewing Co.	Tacoma	WA	191-196, 521-522, 544	1952-58
Heileman, G., Brewing Co.	LaCrosse	WI	197, 291, 530, 647	1937-40
Henry F. Ortlieb Brewing Co.	Philadelphia	PA	298-299, 623	1933-89
Hensler, Joseph, Brewing Co.	Newark	NJ	198	1935-58
Highland Brewing Co.	Springfield	MA	199	1894-98
Hofbrau Brewing Co.	Allentown	PA	200	1933-73
Hohenadel, John, Brewery	Philadelphia	PA	523	1933-52
Horlacher Brewing Co.	Allentown	PA	204	1933-78
Hudepohl Brewing Co.	Cincinnati	OH	205-211, 606	1933-89
Hull Brewing Co.	New Haven	CT	524	1933-67
Hyde Park Breweries Assn.	St. Louis	MO	525	1933-54
Iroquois Beverage Corp.	Buffalo	NY	214-219	1933-55
Jackson Brewing Co.	New Orleans	LA	220-221	1938-66
Jacob Leinenkugel Brewing Co.	Chippewa Falls	WI	565-568	1933-
Jacob Ruppert	New York	NY	366-368	1933-66
Jacob Schmidt Brewing Co.	St. Paul	MN	378, 501	1955-72
James Hanley Co.	Providence	RI	186-189, 467, 520, 563	1933-51
John Hohenadel Brewery	Philadelphia	PA	523	1933-52
Jones Brewing Co.	Smithton	PA	400-403, 461, 487	1952-
Jos. Schlitz Brewing Co.	Milwaukee	WI	371-377	1933-89
Joseph Hensler Brewing Co.	Newark	NJ	198	1935-58
Jung, Wm. G., Brewing Co.	Random Lake	WI	469	1934-58
Kamm & Schellinger Co.	Mishawaka	IN	470, 564	1933-52
King's Brewery	Cleveland	OH	222	1939-41
Kingsbury Breweries	Sheboygan	WI	526	1934-70
Koch, Fred, Brewery	Dunkirk	NY	22, 607	1973-89
Krantz Brewing Corporation	Findlay	OH	269-271	1933-56
Krueger, G., Brewing Co.	Newark	NJ	608-609	1933-60
Kuebler Brewing Co.	Easton	PA	224	1933-52
Lacrosse Breweries	LaCrosse	WI	641	1933-55
Largay Brewing Co.	Waterbury	CT	347	1934-49
Latrobe Brewing Co.	Latrobe	PA	357-365, 534-535	1937-
Lebanon Valley Brewing Co.	Lebanon	PA	480	1952-58
Leinenkugel, Jacob, Brewing Co.	Chippewa Falls	WI	565-568	1933-
Leisy Brewing Co.	Cleveland	OH	225	1933-61
Lemp, Wm. J., Brewing Co.	East St. Louis	IL	226, 473	1939-42
Liebmann Breweries	New York	NY	236, 355-356, 533	1933-46
Lion Brewery of New York City	New York	NY	227-230, 610	1933-41
Lion Inc., The	Wilkes-Barre	PA	154-155	1934-80
Lone Star Brewing Co.	San Antonio	TX	233-234, 569, 611	1941-70
Los Angeles Brewing Co	Los Angeles	CA	460, 475	1934-54
Louis F. Neuweiler's Sons	Allentown	PA	260, 621	1951-68
Lucky Lager Brewing Co.	San Francisco	CA	474, 527	1948-64
Maier Brewing Co.	Los Angeles	CA	444, 556, 668	1951-71
Meister Brau	Chicago	IL	612	1967-72
Metz Brewing Co.	Omaha	NE	613-618	1939-61
Michael, C & J	LaCrosse	WI	113	1910-18
Miller Brewing Co.	Milwaukee	WI	231-232, 240-251, 528-529	1920-

Brewery	City	State	Photo Reference Numbers	In Business
Minneapolis Brewing Co.	Minneapolis	MN	429, 518	1953-67
Minnesota Brewing Co.	St. Paul	MN	316	1995-
Mound City Brewing Co.	New Athens	IL	338	1933-51
My Brewing Co.	Omaha	NE	619	1959-63
Narragansett Brewing Co	Cranston	RI	254	1933-66
National Brewing Co.	Baltimore	MD	255-259, 476, 570, 620	1938-93
Neuweiler's, Louis F., Sons	Allentown	PA	260, 621	1951-68
North Bay Brewing Co.	Santa Rosa	CA	441	1948-58
Oertel Brewing Co.	Louisville	KY	261-265, 571-573, 622	1934-68
Old Reading Brewery	Reading	PA	281-285	1933-69
Olympia Brewing Co.	Tumwater	WA	669	1933-
Ortlieb, Henry F., Brewing Co.	Philadelphia	PA	298-299, 623	1933-89
Oshkosh Brewing Co.	Oshkosh	WI	82-83, 448-449, 593-594	1938-71
Otto Erlanger Brewing Co.	Philadelphia	PA	115	1942-50
Pabst Brewing Co.	Milwaukee	WI	14, 301-310, 531	1933-
Pacific Malting and Brewing Co.	San Jose	CA	427	1933-52
Pearl Brewing Co.	San Antonio	TX	315	1972-
Peter Breidt Brewing Co.	Elizabeth	NJ	56	1933-51
Peter Fox Brewing Co.	Chicago	IL	141-142	1933-55
Peter Hand Brewery	Chicago	IL	624	1933-88
Pfeiffer Brewing Co.	Detroit	MI	317-324, 532, 670	1948-72
Phoenix Brewing Co.	Bay City	MI	325-326	1933-51
Piels Bros	Brooklyn	NY	328-333, 625, 642	1933-73
Pilsen Brewing Co.	Chicago	IL	549-551	1934-63
Pilsener Brewing Co.	Hazelton	PA	190, 300, 411, 479	1933-50
Pioneer Brewing Co.	Aberdeen	WA	335	1933-44
Pittsburgh Brewing Co.	Pittsburgh	PA	253, 468, 545-546, 548	1934-70
Poth Brewing Co.	Philadelphia	PA	336	1940-41
Potosi Brewing Co.	Potosi	WI	2	1933-72
Queen City Brewing Co.	Cumberland	MD	274-278	1940-74
Rahr Green Bay Brewing Co	Green Bay	WI	279-280	1934-53
Red Top Brewing Co.	Cincinnati	OH	348-351	1933-56
Regal Pale Brewing Co.	San Francisco	CA	352, 547	1953-62
Renner Co.	Youngstown	OH	353-354, 575	1935-62
Rochester Brewing Co.	Rochester	NY	412	1953-56
Ruppert, Jacob	New York	NY	366-368	1933-66
San Antonio Brewing Assn.	San Antonio	TX	315	1933-52
San Francisco Brewing Corp.	San Francisco	CA	72-74	1935-57
Schaefer, F & M, Brewing Co	Brooklyn	NY	369	1933-78
Scheidt, Adam, Brewing Co.	Norristown	PA	337, 418, 584-585	1945-60
Schell, August, Brewing Co.	New Ulm	WI	370, 627	1933-
Schlitz, Jos., Brewing Co.	Milwaukee	WI	371-377	1933-89
Schmidt Brewing Co.	Detroit	MI	483, 671	1933-53
Schmidt, C. & Sons	Philadelphia	PA	379-385, 536	1933-88
Schmidt, Jacob, Brewing Co.	St. Paul	MN	378, 501	1955-72
Schoenling Brewing Co.	Cincinnati	OH	537, 579-581	1934-84
Schott Brewing Co.	Highland	IL	386	1933-40
Sebewaing Brewing Co.	Sebewaing	MI	387-391	1933-64
Sicks Brewing Co	Salem	OR	484, 538, 591	1944-53
Sicks Rainier Brewing Co.	Seattle	WA	339-346, 481-482, 626	1956-69
Standard Brewing Co.	Cleveland	OH	114, 395, 413, 486, 597-601, 628-629, 648	1933-61
Star Peerless Brewing	Belleville	IL	582	1933-57
Sterling Brewers	Evansville	IN	396-399	1933-72
Storck Products Co.	Slinger	WI	404	1935-45
Stroh Brewing Co.	Detroit	MI	405-408	1933-85
Terre Haute Brewing Co.	Terre Haute	IN	447, 500	1935-58
Theo Hamm's Brewing Co.	St. Paul	MN	172-184, 605, 640, 646	1933-75
Tivoli Brewing Co.	Denver	CO	410, 630-631	1933-69
United Breweries	Chicago	IL	67	1909-17
United States Brewing Co.	Chicago	IL	576	1936-48
Vienna Brewing Co.	Cincinnati	OH	420-421	1933-41
Weber Waukesha Brewing Co.	Waukesha	WI	488-489	1934-58
Wehle Brewing Co.	West Haven	CT	422-424, 632	1933-43
West Bend Lithia	West Bend	WI	293	1936-72
West End Brewing Co.	Utica	NY	414-417	1933-70
William Simon Brewery	Buffalo	NY	393	1933-73
Wm. G. Jung Brewing Co.	Random Lake	WI	469	1934-58
Wm. Gerst Brewing Co.	Nashville	TN	555	1949-51
Wm. Gretz Brewing Co.	Philadelphia	PA	466	1935-60
Wm. J. Lemp Brewing Co.	East St. Louis	IL	226, 473	1939-42
Wooden Shoe Brewing Co.	Minster	OH	428, 490-492	1939-53
Worcester Brewing Co.	Worcester	MA	583	1945-62
Wunderbrau Brewing Co.	Cincinnati	OH	430	1951-56
Yankee Brewing Co.	New York	NY	431	1957-65
Yoerg Brewing Co.	St. Paul	MN	432	1933-52